Monograph 17
AMERICAN ETHNOLOGICAL SOCIETY

WARRIORS PERFORMING CEREMONIAL IN BALL COURT
(CODEX NUTTALL, FOL. 80)

(Courtesy Worcester Art Museum)

CLAY MODEL OF BALL GAME, TARASCAN STYLE

MONOGRAPHS OF THE
AMERICAN ETHNOLOGICAL SOCIETY
Edited by Marian W. Smith

17

THEODORE STERN

THE RUBBER-BALL GAMES
OF THE AMERICAS

UNIVERSITY OF WASHINGTON PRESS

SEATTLE AND LONDON

Acknowledgments

Whatever the final merit of this paper may be, it has profited greatly from the advice and assistance of a number of individuals. From its inception it has been at once sustained and searchingly criticized by Dr. Linton Satterthwaite, under whose supervision it was written. Dr. Frank G. Speck likewise gave of his mature judgment and it is with deep regret that I realize he cannot see the finished product. To Dr. Julian H. Steward I am indebted for valuable criticisms and for special courtesies. Drs. J. Alden Mason, Alfred Métraux, and Gordon F. Ekholm have given freely of their time and knowledge, with results that I can only hope are perceptible in the text. Dr. A. Irving Hallowell read the final draft and offered suggestions that have been incorporated where possible. In addition, permission to utilize unpublished materials was kindly granted by Matthew W. Stirling, Carl Ruppert, J. S. Bolles, A. L. Smith (subject to confirmation of the Carnegie Institution of Washington), J. M. Corbett, John M. Cooper, and the Rev. Willard R. Elton. Finally, Drs. Eduardo Noguera, Jens Yde, John Gillin, and Irving Rouse, as well as the officials of the Gothenburg Ethnographical Museum, and the Worcester Art Museum, gave me assistance within their various fields.

It is no exaggeration to say that this paper would have been meagre indeed, if not totally impossible of execution, without the contributions of these men. For what I have done with the materials, the final state to which the paper has been brought, I alone am responsible.

An additional word should be added as to the circumstances under which this study appears. Originally entered as a doctoral dissertation before the Department of Anthropology, University of Pennsylvania, in 1948, it appears now by virtue of the generous support accorded it by both the Philadelphia Anthropological Society and the American Ethnological Society. The debt under which their kindness places me is one I record with distinct pleasure.

January 29, 1948.   Theodore Stern
Eugene, Oregon.

TABLE OF CONTENTS

MAPS

CHAPTER ONE

Introduction

As the Spanish explorers began to return from the first voyages of discovery in the New World, they bore with them many a tale of strange new wonders witnessed beyond the seas. Among the marvels was a ball of remarkable resilience, with which the islanders of Hispaniola played a game akin to tennis or *pallone*. Columbus himself brought back such a ball, probably from his second voyage. "... Before I came here," wrote Las Casas long afterwards from New Spain, "I saw one, as big as a small jug, which the old Admiral brought to Seville."[1]

It was not long before the advancing fortunes of the conquerors swept them on to the mainland and to the overthrow of Mexico. Here once more they found the rubber-ball game, in a form which they readily recognized as related to that of the Antilles.[2] Further expansion, in Middle and South America, served to bring to light still other versions of the game. By 1745, it was possible for Father Gumilla to supplement a description of the Otomac game which he had witnessed on the Orinoco with a citation from a fellow Jesuit, Father Rojas, for the Acaxee of far-off Sinoloa. Father Gilij, who followed him, was able to add to these examples the data of Abbot Clavigero for central Mexico and for the Tarahumare and other north Mexican peoples, as well as the account of Oviedo for the Antilles. Similar instances were adduced by the editor of Father Eder's description of the Mojo, which was published in Budapest. Nor was the knowledge confined to the ranks of the learned clergy, for we find the Antillean, Otomac, and Mexican games treated together in the letters of that distinguished 18th century traveller, Count Carli.[3]

In affirming the genetic relationship of these rubber-ball games, modern anthropologists are thus taking no very novel stand. Since, however, they have been able to bring to bear on the subject the accumulated knowledge of the intervening centuries, their conclusions are welcome confirmation. The most important contribution of recent times has been the research of Baron Erland Nordenskiöld, who assembled the known data pertaining to the various versions of the game, including the results of his own field-work, and drew broad conclusions from their distri-

[1] Las Casas, 1909, p. 159.
[2] Motolinia, 1903, p. 337; Martyr, p. 469.
[3] Gumilla, vol. 1, p. 108; Gilij, vol. 2, p. 272; Eder, p. 343f; Carli, vol. 2, pp. 16—20.

bution.[4] His study has, in turn, stimulated the reporting of further instances of the game, both among present-day peoples and in the accounts preserved in early sources. Theoretical discussions, moreover, have come to place increasing emphasis upon the game as a trait present in both of the Americas.

In view of these developments, it has been thought worthwhile to assemble all the known data pertaining to the game and to submit them to as rigorous an examination as lies in my power, in order to review previous statements in the light of the additional information, and to synthesize present knowledge as a basis for future study. In particular, the stable elements of the game will be investigated, and the natural and social environments affecting the spread of the game will be the subject of inquiry.

While archeological evidence has received full consideration in the ensuing discussion, it is planned to reserve a detailed analysis of the Middle American and Antillean ball courts for a separate paper. Accordingly, they receive less emphasis here.

While the descriptive data which form the body of this study lie patent to the view and are thus easily capable of check, the underlying premises which govern their treatment are far less obvious. Yet the latter, to my mind, likewise merit being brought forth into the light of day; for if some of them, as hypotheses, receive careful scrutiny herein, others retain a quasi-axiomatic status, as representing conditions which though subject to exception, appear as a rule to be true. Perhaps the most satisfactory way to indicate the character of some of these assumptions is to review briefly the development of the present report.

It has long been the practice to equate together all games played with rubber balls, and this became my initial assumption. Bit by bit, I was forced to abandon it, as it became increasingly clear that they fall, virtually without exception, into two general categories. The first shares with lacrosse, shinny, and the kicking race in North America and with hockey in South America, competition between two teams; while the second, designated here as the "circle game" from the ring formed by the participants, resembles most closely the shuttlecock and maize-leaf-ball games of South America in its non-team characteristics. Indeed, as we shall see, the parallels within competitive games on the one hand and circle games on the other go beyond mere details of play. If, however, one compares the features of the two categories of game in the instances that follow, it will be found that the rubber ball is not only the chief element held in common but almost the sole one. The measure of their relationship is accordingly examined in the concluding section.

Further investigation indicated that within limits traits might be given relative weighting, and that such heretic action might prove fruit-

[4] Nordenskiöld, 1920, pp. 101—9.

ful. The singling out of the rubber ball as a primary element for comparison arises from considerations of native linguistic usage. In the majority of cases in which the etymology of the native name for the game could be secured, it was found to contain the element for "ball," either linked or synonymous with that for "rubber." (These were for competitive forms of the game; no terms could be found for the circle type). Other features have proved more recalcitrant toward ranking. In general, it has been assumed here that methods of striking the ball, and to a lesser extent manner of play – that is to say, learned bodily behavior – may more readily overstep the threshold of cultural difference than such complex features as structural ball courts and religious associations. For purposes of comparison they have accordingly been regarded as more fundamental to the game. I should be reluctant, however, to raise this approach to the level of generality without further substantial proof.

Cognate to these concerns is the relationship between each type of rubber-ball game and a prototypic form from which it might have derived. Ball play is universal in the Americas and several games already cited evince striking similarities to one or the other class of rubber-ball game.[5] It is probable that some of the features shared by the contemporary games derive from a common ancestral sport but some may arise through convergence and some may represent borrowing at no very distant time. The assessment of these factors has proven far from simple; nor can a final answer be expected.

On a broad plane, it is a matter of considerable interest, once the instances of the rubber-ball games have been caught up in a web of resemblances, to determine the forces that have been operative in bringing about the distribution as it is known today. In part, ecological factors may have been operative, a matter examined in the following and the final sections. The cultural background of the receiving society may also have played a part, although here the arguments are chiefly inferential. Finally, purely historical considerations of space and time may be involved. Since so many variables are at work, the spatiotemporal postulate of "age-area" must be applied with great discretion. In this connection, Cooper's judgment can scarcely be bettered, "that with proper safeguards and techniques a good deal of reconstruction is nevertheless possible, though in such reconstruction reasonable probability, rather than certainty, is all that can as a rule be hoped for or attained."[6] An additional reservation obtains in the application of the hypothesis to South American data, since we know that there in particular the

---

[5] For North America, see Culin. Distributional data for South America have been presented by Nordenskiöld (1919, 1920 in particular), and in Cooper, 1949. References to reports on specific games are given in the concluding section.

[6] Cooper, 1946a, p. 295.

distribution of elements has been profoundly modified by large-scale migrations.

In its development, as outlined above, the present study has relinquished what seems to be an over-simplified approach for one that, at the other extreme, is threatened by an almost overwhelming complexity. If it therefore furnishes no immediate answer, at least it probably lies closer to an ultimate solution. On this point the reader must be the final judge.

In considering the native occurrences of the rubber-ball game, no attempt is made in the first chapters to discuss the specific culture areas within which they fall. They are arranged in geographical order. Starting with the Otomac of Venezuela, attention falls in turn upon the tribes toward the south, in Colombia, Ecuador, and western Brazil, to work north once more in the eastern part of that country until the Guianas are reached. Discussion then turns to the circum-Carribbean, to the manifestations of the game both in the Antilles and on the mainland. The game of the Maya is next considered, then that of the southern and central Mexican peoples, followed by those of the northern Mexican tribes, and finally those of the American Southwest.

It is not entirely chance, or even the obvious need to start somewhere that leads me to begin with the Otomac. We have several independent, detailed accounts of their game which present an unambiguous picture, and therefore offer a standard for comparison when more fragmentary descriptions for other South American tribes are taken up. The Otomac game may serve as a keystone to any synthesis because, to anticipate subsequent analysis, it stands midway between those of the Antilles and the remainder of the tribes of South America. Our other conclusions are reserved for a final chapter.

Distribution of Rubber

Whatever may have been the nature of the sports that formed its prototype, the rubber-ball game owes many distinctive characteristics of play to the resilient quality of the ball. The invention of a bounding ball together with its subsequent introduction into an existing game in all probability took place through experimentation in an area where rubber was already known and its technology familiar: it is most likely that the development took place within the locus of native, rubber-bearing flora. Furthermore, it might be expected that the same natural distribution might in measure have been effective in restricting and channeling the subsequent diffusion of the game. Consequently, the geographical incidence of the game must be projected against the occurrence of indigenous sources of rubber.

There are a number of plants and trees which produce rubber, usually in an aqueous (latex) suspension, and most of them can be exploited satisfactorily for native needs by much the same method. Although they are most abundant within the tropical rain forests, they are by no means limited to that zone. In general, it may be said that sources of rubber are available from the American Southwest almost to the northern limits of the Gran Chaco of Argentina and roughly to the 25th parallel in Brazil. They are not present in the plateaus of the Andean highlands, though they are present on the eastern slopes. The chief members of this group are as follows:

Hevea (Siphonia). Family: *Euphorbiaceae.* Of approximately ten species of Para rubber trees, *H. brasiliensis* is the most important. It flourishes in low, recurrently inundated land, though it is found at altitudes up to 2100—3300 feet. Range: the Amazon basin, including parts of eastern Peru and the lower courses of the main rivers tributary to the Amazon, as well as that river itself. Representatives of this genus are also found in the valley of the Paraguay and, to the north, in the Guianas.

Castilla (or *Castilloa*). Family: *Artocarpaceae.* Members of the *Castilla* are present in the Amazon basin only on the upper courses of tributaries of the great river *(C. elastica)*, in lowland Ecuador (the native name, *heve*, given it by the natives of Esmeraldas was later transferred to the Para rubber tree), and northward through Middle America into the *tierra caliente* of Mexico. In Panama, both *C. markamiana (Perebea* sp.) and *C. panamensis* bear the local native name, *ule.* Lloyd (1911, p. 5) assumes that the *ulequahuitl,* the latex-producing tree of aboriginal Mexico, was probably of this genus.

A related plant on the slopes of eastern Peru is *Olmedia,* represented there by two species, *O. aspera* and *O. laevis.*

Sapium (Murunda, Micranda), also of the *Euphorbiaceae,* is found along the tributaries and course of the middle Amazon, reaching westward to the Andes, where it grows at altitudes up to 6—8000 feet. To the north, *S. jenmani* or *S. cladogyne* are cited as sources used by the natives of the Guianas.

Hancornia. Family: *Apocynaceae.* Several varieties of *Hancornia* exist but five of the principal species have been subsumed under one name, *H. speciosa.* The proper environment of this genus is the arid terrain, sandy and rocky, of the tablelands of Brazil, at altitudes often exceeding 3300 feet. *Hancornia* thus ranges along the *campos cerrados* and *catingas* of the eastern Brazilian highlands from Sao Paolo in the south to Maranhao and Piauhy in the north. Still farther to the north, an otherwise unspecified liana of the *Apocynaceae* was mentioned by Barrère in 1743 as the source of rubber used by the aborigines of French Guiana. Finally, in the southwestern United States, Indian hemp, *Apocynum,* is cited as a potential rubber-producer.

Manihot is yet another member of the family of *Euphorbiaceae* which yields a wild rubber. *M. glaziovii, M. dichotoma,* and *M. heptaphylla* constitute the three principal species that possess this property. *Manihot glaziovii* occurs in the more arid sections of the eastern Brazilian states of Ceará, Piauhy, and Bahia. Hydrocyanic acid in the rubber restricts somewhat the uses to which it can be put. The resin is the "Ceará" of commerce.

Guayule (Parthenium argentatum) (Family: *Compositae*) is only one of eight species to be found among the members of the desert shrub vegetation of northern Mexico and the southwestern United States, south to Puebla. In Querétaro, *P. incanum* and *P. lyratum* are classed together by the Otomí(?) under the name, *tatanini*, and still yield rubber to the country youths. *P. argentatum*, which grows at altitudes between 6—8000 feet, is a perennial producing a rubber free from latex. In some regions, and especially in Durango, it is said to have long been a source of rubber, extracted by chewing the bark of the shrub, and then made into balls. The first information as to the use and properties of this plant is attributed to a Jesuit, Father Negrete, in the middle of the eighteenth century. The native name is derived by Seler from *quauh* (wood, tree, or forest) plus *olli* (rubber).

Finally, mention may be made of members of the milkweeds *(Asclepiadaceae)*, in particular *Asclepias subulata* and *A. erosa* of the deserts of southern California and Arizona, *Jatropha*, *Pedilanthus* (both of the *Euphorbiaceae*), and *Plumieria* (Family: *Apocynaceae*) of Mexico as rubber-producers that may have been exploited in aboriginal times. For the Guianas, in addition to *Hevea*, Appun (vol. 2, p. 153) reports ficoids (Family: *Moraceae*) of the genus *Urostigma*. Since the ficoids are prevailingly Asiatic in occurrence, this identification is probably erroneous.[7]

For native purposes the small quantities of rubber required could be supplied by most of the flora exploited, by the simple method of slashing stem, roots, or leaves and collecting the latex that oozed forth. The water was then evaporated and the rubber coagulated by letting it stand, a process hastened by the action of fire or by the addition of special herbs. There is little doubt that the similarity of technique over wide areas was permitted by the presence, in so many rubber-bearing genera, of a latex, that is to say, of a colloidal suspension of rubber in water.[8] It was only in such flora as *guayule*, which lacks latex, that a different method had to be employed to extract the gum.

Throughout most of its range, rubber is thus accessible through a relatively simple technology. Moreover, the finished product, the rubber ball, was traded beyond the limits of natural distribution. In central Mexico, tribute exacted by Montezuma from the lowland tribes included some 16,000 of these objects each year.[9] At the other extreme, the Chané, on the Rio Parapití, just north of the Gran Chaco, lie below the boundary of native rubber, and consequently were dependent upon neighboring tribes for supply. A legend which Nordenskiöld cites in evidence deals with attempts to fetch, first a white, then a black, rubber ball from the north.[10]

---

[7] See, Denis, Pt. 1; Goode; Shelford. See also: Altamirano; Barker; Barrère; Bello; Cook; Hall and Long; Lloyd; Roth; Whitbeck.

[8] Conant, pp. 76—81, discusses the chemistry of rubber. See also pertinent sections in Cook, Jumelle, and Lloyd.

[9] Codex Mendoza: tribute list, Clavigero, p. 405f.

[10] Nordenskiöld, 1920, p. 102.

The Antilles form yet another region which has often been represented as lacking in rubber; but this view appears to be erroneous. There are grounds for believing that a native source was present and that it was exploited in aboriginal times.[11]

With few exceptions, then, it can be said that the occurrence of the rubber-ball game was largely coterminous with that of native rubber; that is to say, the former had not spread appreciably beyond the range of natural supply.

On the other hand, the game is not reported from vast tracts within the middle and lower course of the Amazon system, together with much of the seaboard of Brazil, despite the presence there of such readily exploited sources of rubber as *Hevea* and *Hancornia*. So striking an absence may be apparent only, and future reports or the publication of old accounts may resolve it. On the other hand, it may have its roots in purely cultural factors. The latter premise will be investigated in detail in the following pages.

[11] Stahl (p. 185) states that, since no rubber-bearing plants existed in the Antilles, Oviedo's description of ball-making may actually have referred to the tribes of the South American mainland, where *Siphonia elastica* (i. e. *Hevea sp.*) is known to have been present. In this point of view he was followed by Fewkes (p. 85) and by Nordenskiöld (1920, p. 108). Lovén, on the other hand, believes that Oviedo's account was correctly ascribed and cites in evidence (p. 412) Ober, *A Guide to the West Indies*, p. 217, to the effect that native rubber is found in the mountain forests of Santo Domingo. If this is not an introduced rubber run wild, it might well have constituted the aboriginal source of supply, as Lovén suggests.

However, the best evidence that can be adduced as to the self-sufficiency of the Antilles in this respect lies in the pages of Las Casas, who lived for years in the islands, and who speaks of a tree growing on Hispaniola (Haiti) and in the *tierras calientes*, from which rubber was obtained. "...No es mucho menos industria," he says (1909, p. 159), "la que tuvieron en hallar las pelotas con que juegan. En esta isla Española y en las tierras calientes se cría un árbol que por no mirar en ello no lo cognoscí, que dándole algunas heridas sale dél una goma por gotas gordas y blancas; destas juntan muchas que luego se pegan y tornan negras como la pez, y hecho un bulto de aquesta goma cuan grande lo quieren hacer, aredondéanlo con una piedra y comunmente lo dejan tan grande como una pelota de viento de las nuestras; ... Habíalas aquí muchas y en todas estas islas......" If, as suggested by this passage, the same tree was present both on Hispaniola and on the mainland familiar to Las Casas, it may well have been a member of the *Castilla*.

CHAPTER TWO

THE RUBBER-BALL GAMES IN SOUTH AMERICA

Otomac (Otomacan linguistic family)[1]

Ball: As large as the Spanish May-ball, or four times the size of the common Italian *(pallone?)* ball, and with a weight of approximately two pounds, the ball employed was solid, dense, elastic, and of the greatest resiliency on the rebound. Gilij had heard that it was made from the resin of a tree native to the land of the Otomac; but he adds that he himself had never seen it growing (Gum, Gil). Bueno mentions the use of the gum for other purposes by the Marquiritare.[2]

Court: Gumilla alludes to a beautiful and very clean *trinquete* (court) in the neighborhood of the town, but somewhat apart from the houses. Gilij states that such a plaza, set aside for the ball game, was to be found in every Otomac town.[3]

Players: All the men not engaged in the work of the day go to the court as soon as their comrades have left, where they commence the game. At midday, the women, having finished their work, join them (Gum, Gil). Both sexes, when playing, wear only enough clothing to cover the private parts (Gil).

Officials: One (Gil) or more (Gum) umpires are selected from among the elders to declare fouls and to pass on disputed points. The official is distinguished by a piece of tiger skin, carried in the hand. How he is chosen is not stated.

---

[1] See: Gumilla (Gum), vol. 1, ch. 11, pp. 107—111; Gilij (Gil), vol. 2, bk. 4, ch. 16, pp. 270—2; Bueno, (B), p. 140f. Prudhomme, p. 156f, and Pons, p. 204f, offer only abridgements of Gumilla.

Gumilla, Gilij, and Bueno served as missionaries to the Otomac and adjacent tribes in a period spanned by approximately half a century. Their eye-witness accounts thus enjoy a certain measure of contemporaneity and, since none of the immediate neighbors of the Otomac is known to have played a similar game, divergencies in our sources must be ascribed, not so much to temporal change or to outside influence, as to local differences.

[2] Bueno, p. 67.

[3] Since in the European game of tennis the word, *trinquete*, bore precise reference to a court in which walls and roof formed a series of angles (Covarrubias Orozco, p. 195), it is tempting to see here an indication of the presence of a structural court, perhaps with walls, comparable to those of the Antilles, of Central America, and of the Mexican area. However, it is likewise possible that the term was applied by Gumilla by way of analogy, rather than in accordance with strict usage, a view which gains confirmation by the practice of his contemporaries of alluding to the native game as a "tennis game."

Teams: Sides are evenly matched, with twelve on each team at the beginning of the game. When the women enter the game, they replace their husbands; but the teams are constantly augmented, so that by evening each side numbers twenty-four (Gum, Gil). Spectators form fervent cheering sections for one side or the other (Gum).

Wagers: The favored wager is a basket of corn; lacking this, strings of glass beads; and, if they do not possess them, then they gamble everything in the house (Gum). Knives and hatchets are mentioned in the time of Gilij. Women bring provisions to bet (Gum). All stakes set aside by the players appear to have been awarded by the umpire to the victors (Gil); but the manner of distribution among them is not reported. Players lose one stake only to return with another for the next game (Gum).

Play: Gumilla states that men used only the right shoulder to strike the ball, in consequence of which a hard callus developed on that portion of the body. Gilij states that both the right shoulder and the head might be employed. Bueno, describing an intercommunity game, specifies not only head and shoulder but also elbows and buttocks, a variance that may possibly be ascribed to local divergency. Should the ball touch any other portion of the body, the offending player (*i. e.* his side) loses a point (Gum). In the ensuing descriptions, I shall designate this play by the term, "body fault." A ball that touches the ground may still be retrieved by the nearest player (for each one has his own position on the court and does not move from it), who dives to recover it with his shoulder (Gum, Gil). When finally the ball lies dead on the court, marking the first point, the players change places.[4] This probably implies the movement of fresh players into the court to replace those wishing to drop out, or to shifts within the court.

Women strike the ball with wooden rackets two feet in length, rounded at the end, and with a blade approximately eleven inches in breadth.[5] These they wield with both hands and with such good effect that those men who receive their volleys, fearing for their shoulders, put their whole back into returning it. As a result, we are told, scarcely a day passes that sees no back broken, an occasion, as Father Gumilla informs us with upcast eyes, "which these hens celebrate with laughter" (p. 108). These are the same valiant females who accompany their spouses in battle to retrieve enemy arrows.

Yet in play, perfect order seems to be maintained; each one keeps his

[4] Gilij's use of the term, "prima le cacce," is used, in all probability, not in the sense of "first game," but of "first chase." In the European games of that day, several chases made up the total score. "Chase" will be more fully explained subsequently (see page 48).

[5] Kirchoff, (1948, p. 443) suggests that these may have been ordinary canoe paddles.

place, and the silence of the players is broken only by the murmurs of applause with which the spectators greet some able stroke (Gum, Gil).

Ceremonial associations: As the sun rises and the day becomes warmer, the players scarify thighs, legs, and arms with sharpened points, working in place and without once taking their eyes off the ball. When enough blood has flowed, the player throws himself into the river to staunch the bleeding (Gum, B). "This entertainment," Father Bueno specifies, "was rather contemplative and not at all profane."[6] Mention is also made of earth-eating by players in the course of the game; but this appears to form part of the larger pattern of geophagy for which the Otomac are famous.

Inter-village games: The games within the community are described as daily affairs, lasting from the time the fishing canoes leave till their return, about four in the afternoon. They are followed by a dance which occupies the evening (Gum).

However, it is evident from the account of Father Bueno that games also took place between different communities, for he describes a match between the Otomac of his mission of Urbana and those of Cunaviche, which also lasted from morning till sunset.

Omagua (Tupi-Guaraní linguistic stock)[7]

From the tree, cau-uchu (Castilla sp.),[8] the Omagua derived a latex which they called Xerantá-amby, or solidifying slime (Mart). From it they made hollow balls (C) with which the youths played (M).

Poimisano and Paragini (Unaffiliated?)[9]

At the mission of San Balthasar de Atabapo, on the river of the same name, von Humboldt observed the rubber-working of the Poimisano. The raw material was a latex which collected about the roots of a tree and which was termed by the Poimisano and Paragini respectively dapicho and zapis. These words, obviously related, are cognate to that

---

[6] P. 140. It is improbable that the scarification is to be interpreted as a solar offering, despite its conjunction with the early course of the sun, since the Otomac pantheon does not appear to have included a solar deity. It is more likely that its purpose was purgative.

[7] Métraux, 1928, p. 213, quoting José Chantre y Herrera, Historia de las Misiones de la Compañia de Jesús en el Marañon español (1637—1767). Madrid, 1901, p. 99: "'Tambien los Indios (de Mainas) se entretienen haciendo de él pelotas que saltan como si fueran de azogue.'"
See: Maroni (M), p. 424; La Condamine (C), p. 76; Martius (Mart), vol. 1, pp. 440f, 717; vol. 2, pp. 400, 407.

[8] See: Cook, p. 373.

[9] See: von Humboldt, vol. 2, p. 344f.

used by Martius and ascribed by him to the Tupian peoples.[10] If this holds true, the latter are presented in the role of vector for the ball game among the Atabapo tribes. Unlike the ball of the Omagua, however, that of the Poimisano is described as solid. Heated over the fire on a spit, the *dapicho* softens, is beaten with a wooden club, and kneaded into balls three to four inches in diameter. The game in which they are employed at the mission is "the Indian game of tennis, which is celebrated among the [Otomac] inhabitants of Urbana and Encaramada."

Witoto, Bora, Muinane and Okaina (Independent linguistic stocks)[11]

Farabee thus describes the Witoto game: "The men and boys also play ball. They make a large rubber ball, *uwika detirowi* (*Uwika*, ball, rubber: *deterowi*, play – p. 150), about six inches in diameter, and all play together around the central plaza. The ball is tossed into the air and must be caught on the knee of the right leg, bounced into the air again, and received in the same way on the other side. The hands must not be used except in guiding the ball to the knee. These ball games between villages last four or five days. They play ball in the afternoon, and dance at night."

Tessmann, describing the same game *("uike")*, states that it occurred only on festival occasions. The rubber ball was struck only with knees, hands, and the top of the feet. The corresponding game played by neighboring tribes was called *amexkaa* (Bora), *tore* (Muinane), and *dioxooxo* (Okaina). In the last named instance, at least, the name of the game is derived from that of the ball *(dioxo)*.

The Witoto game, according to Tessmann, marks the full moon in the lunar cycle, a symbolization which, however, has taken on an extraneous character in the harvest festival, in which the ball becomes the representation of the fruits of the harvest. As actually observed, the game seems chiefly to occur in the latter context, and the play itself is only part of the entire festival, of which the evening dance is another. Support for its ultimate lunar associations appears to rest primarily upon the fact that the players are termed "Moon people."

In Witoto mythology, Preuss records a contest upon the ball court, in which one of the heavenly deities is decapitated by the ball and is

[10] Martius, vol. 1, p. 440: "Tapicho (richtiger Tapichügh d. h. tief aus der Erde)..." Vol. 2, p. 407: "*Tapicho* (Alto Amazonas) Resina fossillis Siphoniae. (an vox tupica ?)" The ending, — *icho*, resembles that of *cau-uchu* (see Omagua. and *manga-ici* (see Guaraní). In the latter example, the meaning is clearly, "mangabeira-gum." A similar etymology is suggested for *tapicho*.

[11] See: Witoto: Farabee, p. 141; Tesmann, pp. 321, 324; Preuss, pp. 75—8, 314 f. The other tribes in Tessmann, as follows: Bora, p. 276; Muiana, p. 335; Okaina, p. 555. General discussion, Tesmann, p. 606. Tesmann's linguistic terms have been simplified.

devoured by his opponents, the forces of evil. Subsequently, his two sons in a second game secure revenge, defeating and destroying their foe.

Tribes of the Uapés-Caquetá Region

In a statement which possibly refers to the modern Cubeo, Goldman observes that "adults play catching games with rubber balls."[12]

Cocama (Tupi-Guaraní linguistic stock)

A game is described, known to the natives only by the Spanish term *pelota* (ball), in which rubber balls are struck back and forth with the knees.[13] This recalls the Witoto and allied games.

Aguano (Quechuaized after the conquest)

"Rubber balls are present, but perhaps imported. They are struck in play with the feet, but also with knees or head."[14]

Nocaman (Panoan linguistic stock)

Rubber balls, *apumayungi*, used in play by striking with the feet, seem to be old.[15]

Araona and Cavina (Takanan linguistic stock)

Araona: During festivals, the Araona play ball "when belting themselves with the bark of a tree, they receive the ball on the belly and, with a strong movement, cause it to rebound."[16]

Cavina: Nordenskiöld observed hollow rubber balls, containing pellets, in use among the Cavina on the Rio Beni. In play, they were tossed from hand to hand; alternatively they might function as rattles. In his earlier paper cited, he illustrates one of the Cavina balls. Of irregular shape, it is flattened – perhaps through storage – so that its diameters vary between five and seven centimeters. The average wall-thickness is three millimeters.[17]

The ball game enters the supernatural beliefs of the Cavina, to whom the wind is a small boy who throws a rubber ball and thus produces thunder.[18]

[12] Goldman, p. 790.
[13] Tessman, 1930, p. 75.
[14] Ibid, p. 262 (my translation).
[15] Ibid, p. 179.
[16] Church, 1912, p. 147. See also Métraux, 1942, p. 41.
[17] Nordenskiöld, 1917, p. 84; 1920, p. 106.
[18] Métraux, 1942, p. 45.

Colorado (Chibchan linguistic stock)[19]

The Colorado Indians of western Ecuador possess, in common with many highland tribes, funerary games which take place during a wake. In one, the corpse is placed in the middle of the room and mourners form two rows on opposite sides. A rubber ball is then put in motion, being thrown by one man to his opposite number, who must catch it and send it back to the next man on the other side. Should a player drop the ball, he must offer brandy to all the others. At times, burning pieces of wood are substituted for the ball.

It is evident that it is not essential to the game for the ball to be of rubber. Hand and bat games with rubber balls are noted for Ecuador by Parsons, in a milieu that is evidently European.[20] In details of play, the Colorado game appears to be historically unrelated to the developments of rubber-ball games elsewhere in South America.

Paressí and Paressí-Kabishi (Arawakan linguistic stock)[21]

Game: The Paressí term the game, *mataná-aríti*, meaning literally, game of the Paressí (Rn, R. P.).

Ball: *(haira, hairaza)*. Made of the sap of the *Mangabeira (Hancornia speciosa)* tree, the Paressí ball is hollow. A layer of latex is laid over a gently concave piece of wood, and when it becomes firm is removed and rolled around until the edges touch and are pinched together with the fingers. Through a small hole, left open for this purpose, the ball is blown up. Then the hole is sealed and the entire surface built up with latex until it reaches the desired thickness (Rn). The finished specimen is some eight inches (twenty cm.) in diameter (Rt), while those of the Paressí-Kabishi are smaller, with a dimension of only nine to eleven cm.

Court *(uihairanikua*, our place to play ball. Par.): It appears that the Paressí games take place in the central plaza of the village, since houses front on it; and it is likely that the Paressí-Kabishi court is at least near the settlement. Photographs from both tribes show only a level, cleared space, the Paressí-Kabishi court evidencing less care in clearing than that of their cognates. No lines or boundaries appear in any of the photographs, nor are any mentioned in the texts. Two poles or stripped trees appear in the background of the Paressí-Kabishi pictures, at about the

---

[19] Karsten, 1924, pp. 151, 152. See also Karsten, 1932.

[20] Parsons, 1945, p. 53, Cf. p. 128.

[21] See: Paressí: Roosevelt (Rt), pp. 191—3; 195, 198, illus. facing p. 194; Roquette-Pinto (R.Po), 145f., 344; Rondon (Rn), pp. 44—5; M. Schmidt (S), 1943, pp. 18—9, 34—5, vocab. *passim*. Unless otherwise specified, Schmidt, 1943, is the source for native terms which are here simplified.

Paressí-Kabishi: M. Schmidt, 1912, p. 174, fig. 20; 1914, pp. 181, 183, fig. 26 (reproduced for comparison as figure 24 of Schmidt, 1943).

center of the long side of the court, but may actually be unassociated with it.

Players: Among the Paressí, men alone are mentioned and depicted as participants, though women and girls are spectators. Schmidt specifies of the Paressí-Kabishi that only adults participate, and his photographs show young males. Similarity is also shown in clothing, for while Roosevelt's pictures and remarks stand as testimony that the Paressí might play fully clothed in shirt, neckerchief, and trousers, he adds that "they soon discarded most of their clothes, coming down to nothing but trousers or a loin-cloth. Two or three of them had their faces stained with red ochre" (p. 195). For the related tribe, Schmidt shows players clad only in what appears to be an optional loin-string.

Officials: The Paressí have a scorer or umpire, whose function it is to keep count of points.

Teams: Sides are equal. For the Paressí, teams may number eight, ten, or more players *(kahairani,* a good ball player). Schmidt's photographs show only about three Paressí-Kabishi youths on a side, but it is probable that the game depicted was only an informal match.

Wagers and inter-village games: Never a festive gathering goes by that does not see a Paressí ball game in progress. Inter-community games seem to take place on these occasions, and wagers run so high that many Paressí lose their last possession, even including their personal clothing and ornaments (Rn).

Play *(ikonaha,* he plays ball): The ball might be struck only with the head. It is served directly off the floor of the court, though the Paressí-Kabishi might build a small sand "tee" to raise it slightly. The server runs forward, throws himself prone, and, with a toss of his head, butts the ball into the air. A member of the opposition returns it in the same manner, after which it usually gains sufficient altitude to be volleyed from a standing position. Among the Paressí, should the ball go out of bounds on either side, it is brought back. It is probable that teammates might strike the ball in succession *(chiueheta,* passing the ball – Par). A point is scored by sending the ball beyond the opposing players; and this suggests the existence of a goal line of some sort. A goal is greeted with shrill cries of triumph by the scoring team; and play is at once resumed. Schmidt implies that the Paressí-Kabishi score a point when the opposing team permits the ball to touch the court. In neither case are we told whether players perform specialized functions, though they apparently do not play in position; nor are we informed of the division of the wager at the end of the game.

The intra-village games of the Paressí seen by Roosevelt took place as a rule in the late afternoon.

Ceremonial associations are specifically denied for the Paressí-Kabishi game by Schmidt. The same appears to be true for that of the Paressí.

In the latter example, however, the popular hold of the game is manifested in two legends.[22] In one, the lunar deity, Káinare, holds a ball game prior to his marriage with his sister, Olo'ialo; while in the second, the divine ancestors come together to take part in a great ball game in which large stakes are ventured.

Mojo (Arawakan linguistic stock)[23]

Game: *nucaepotò*, to play ball.

Ball (*nePoto*, cf. Taino *batey*): Both a solid and a hollow ball are described. In the former, the resin of a tree is modeled into a sphere, rolled roughly into shape, and finally trimmed with a knife (Eder). The weight of the finished article is given by both authorities as twenty-five pounds.[24]

In the manufacture of the hollow ball, a clay core is first made. When dry, it is coated with the milky resin of the tree. The ball is then dipped into water and the clay dissolved and expressed, doubtless through a cut made in the rubber. The resulting hollow sphere is next inflated and its weight increased by additional coats of latex. Exposed to the sun, it is turned, so that it shall not harden unevenly. Meanwhile, pains are taken to smooth out inequalities, and small amounts of occluded liquid are removed through cuts. The final ball, very carefully smoothed, is said to have weighed approximately five ounces (Eder).

Play: Two forms of ball game are played. In the first, only the solid ball is employed. Two teams, probably equally matched, face each other across an interval of eight paces (about twenty-four feet); and begin to volley the ball with foot or lower leg. As a protection some players wrap a protective bandage about the lower leg, while others ostentatiously leave it off and let the leg become swollen through play. The ball is received, right knee resting on the ground, and sent back with the leg. Players are careful not to strike an opponent in the face with the ball, for this would draw blood and start fights. As they become warmed up, the teams withdraw, keeping the ball in play, to a distance of forty paces (about 120 feet) or more, when they begin to strike the ball, no longer with the leg, but with the head. The ball, however, is

[22] Schmidt, 1945, pp. 19, 228—34, 263 et. seq.

[23] See: Marban, pp. 261, 303, 581 (linguistic terms only); Eder, bk. 5, ch. 5, pp. 341—3; Gilij, vol. 2, bk. 4, *Note*, pp. 385—7, quoting Abbot Emmanuele Iraisòs, with additional remarks.

[24] Since they give an identical weight, there may have been some interdependence between their accounts. Iraisòs is said by Gilij to have been a missionary "worthy of the greatest faith." Eder, as we know, based his account upon observations he himself had made among the Mojo. Nonetheless, when we consider the frequent fatalities arising among other peoples from the use of a ball weighing two pounds or so, the Mojo figure becomes suspect.

not received directly, but is permitted to strike the ground and is then taken on the rebound. Method of scoring, unfortunately, is not mentioned; but from the details of the second game, related below, it is probable that the failure of a team to return the ball counted as a point for the opposition. That a point did not constitute the entire game is clear from the remark that games between "nations" might last for hours. We lack information as to the existence of wagers.[25]

In the second, and less strenuous, game the hollow ball was employed. Players form a circle, kicking the ball into the air with their feet and endeavoring to keep it aloft (Eder). Iraisòs, whose remarks apply specifically to the Kanichana, a linguistically unrelated tribe (see below) settled at the Mojo missions, states that the players are eight, ten or twelve in number, and that they strike the ball with the foot, with the lower leg, or the knee alone. When adults play, they use the solid, twenty-five pound ball, and form a circle only twenty spans (about fifteen feet) in diameter. The youths, employing the small (hollow?) ball, form a larger circle.

This game, like the team game, could be dangerous. Iraisòs saw a ball break the leg of an Indian who was some distance from the scene of the game. He saw another kill an Indian woman.

Kanichana (Unaffiliated). Mòvima (Unaffiliated), Kayuvava (?) (Unaffiliated). Itonama (Unaffiliated), and Baure (Arawakan)

It is uncertain whether the allusion is to the team game or the circle game of the Mojo. But the same game is common among the Movìma, Cujubambi (Kayuvava?), Baurè, Itonama, and Kanichana.

"Il giuoco della palla di ragia, dic' egli, è molto in uso presso le varie nazioni, di cui son composto le missioni de' *Mossi*. Benchè più de' chiamati *Mossi*, affezionati sieno a codesta forta di giuoco i *Canisianài*: I giuocatori son otto, dieci, oppur dodici; e messisi in circolo, ribattono con abilità incredibile la palla, ora col pie, ora colla polpa delle gambe, ed ora pure colle ginocchia. Gli

[25] Eder, p. 341f. "In duas deinde turmas intervallo octo passuum se dividunt, & pilam pede, vel tibia in adversam turmam propellunt; tibiam vero alii fascia quadam obvolvunt, alii ostentationis causa nuda, ac idcirco fœde intumescente utuntur. Adversarius pilam exceptam flexo dextro poplite terræ allidit ope tibiæ atque ita remittit. Cavent autem solicite, ne in vultum cujusquam incidat, ac sanguinem pondere, & impetu eliciat. Cum ludendo nonnihil inardescunt, ad quadraginta, & amplius, passus a se recedunt, & rem non jam tibiis, sed capitibus gerunt, pilam tamen ante in terram incidere, ac inde in altum subsilire sinunt, & capite inter relabendum exceptam parti adversae remittunt. Lusus ut ut violentus in horas protrahitur, maxime si partes ludo indulgentes diversis constent nationibus de palma con certantibus."

Cf. Métraux, 1942, p. 73, for an interpretation of the preceding passage that differs in certain details from that presented here.

adulti usano di palla solida, e grande a tal segno, che quella da me veduta, con qui ordinariamente giuocavano, era del peso di 25. libbre Spagnuole. I giovanetti però le usan piccole, e per lo più vote al die dentro.

Questo medesimo giuoco è commune tra *Mobìmi*, e *Cujubambi*, e *Baùri*, e *Itonàmi*; ma i più eccellenti giuocatore di palla, e quei, che più la frequentano, sono i *Piccoli* [Chiquitos], i quali la ribattono colla testa, o cogli omeri. Ho anche inteso da un ex-missionario del *Paraguai*, che i *Guaranesi*... tra' quali è molto usata codella palla, si servono per resospingerla, di piedi, e gambe, e ginocchi, appunto come i *Mossi*...."[26]

Chiquito (Chiquitoan linguistic family)[27]

Game: D'Orbigny calls it *Guatoroch*, and in a footnote adds that the same name serves for the tree which produces the rubber, as well as the rubber itself. Carbajal, speaking of the trees of the province, mentions the *vatoviras*, which seems to be the same tree.

Ball: From the rubber tree, so the latter explains, the natives derive the latex, spreading it out upon their bodies and leaving it there until it solidifies, when they remove the band thus formed and wind it up into a spherical form. The ball thus seems to have been solid.

The status of the game appears to have changed somewhat with the passage of time. Fernandez alludes to it as one of several sports indulged in after the midday meal. More than a hundred years later, d'Orbigny found it the old national sport, kept up in the whole province where it was played primarily on feast days. Since the latter has left us a detailed description of the game he witnessed, I can do no better than to offer a translation of it. All footnotes are mine.

"At three o'clock a barbarous music told me of the arrival of the players. It was one of the two sides, composed of twenty-five to thirty natives bearing in triumph a great bundle of corn cobs, reserved to mark the gaining side.[28] The Indians were accompanied by musicians, some beating a tambourine, others shaking a calabash filled with little stones, while others played upon a pipe made of a long cane, like a flute, pierced with two holes so near the end that the musician had to stretch his arms at full length to draw sounds from it. All danced about the bundle of corn, going into contortions and assuming the most extraordinary attitudes. The opposing side soon arrived with a like musical [accompaniment] and assumed postures just as grotesque. The two sides jeered a long time at each other, walking about the great court of the school.[29] They proceeded to the nomination of players charged with serving the ball for each [side]. Some judges traced two lines which were to serve as boundaries for the players; the latter then took their places on each side, in such manner that their heads would be in the most favorable position

[26] Iraisòs, quoted in Gilij, vol. 2, bk. 4, *Note*, p. 387.
[27] See: Fernandez, p. 37; Carbajal, p. 25; d'Orbigny, 1845, pp. 36—9; Nordenskiöld, 1920, p. 104; Iraisòs in Gilij, vol. 2, bk. 4, *Note*, p. 387.
[28] Adam and Henry list the word, *yabare-z*, cualquier cosa con que cuentan en el juego de la pelota; anything with which they keep score in the ball game.
[29] In the time of Fernandez, the game took place in the great plaza. Central location is implied in both statements.

to receive the ball.[30] The first row crouched to recover the shots that skimmed along the ground, while the others formed rows behind them, ranged according to height. The drums and music of the two parties announced the beginning of the struggle. The Indian chosen to serve the ball for his side danced a long time, turning to the sound of the music.[31] As he leaped in this manner, he threw the ball to the ground and sent it with a stroke of his forehead to his side, who sent it back, likewise with the head, to the opposing side, who had to return it in the same way, until one of the two sides failed.[32] Then the gaining side received a corn cob in token of its point, and jeered at its rivals. The side which, in the course of a day's intense contest, succeeded in winning the most corn cobs, was proclaimed victorious. It had won exclusive right to drink chicha, which had been prepared at common expense, and to taunt the vanquished freely."

The suspicion, raised by the foregoing account, that the lines of rivalry were clearly drawn and of relative stability gains support from a statement made by the same author in another context. In the Chiquito game, he affirms, "half of the inhabitants of a village pit themselves against the other;"[33] and little is lacking to complete a picture of permanent sportive rivalries based upon a moiety dichotomy.

Churápa (Chiquitoan linguistic family)[34]

Mention is made of a bat and ball game. In addition, there formerly existed a game, played with rubber balls, which were hit back and forth with the head. It bore the local name, táurósh. It seems likely that the latter game, the name and details of which agree with Chiquitan gautoroch, is indeed to be identified with it.

Chané (Arawakan linguistic stock)[35]

The Indians, we are told, played ball with their heads in place of the racquets used in tennis, and played as skillfully as could the Spaniards with their racquets. Nordenskiöld himself saw Chané boys on the Rio Parapití playing headball, the native name for which is toki. A legend which he relates has reference to the ball game and, according to him, reflects the necessity of importing the balls from the north. Both a white ball (toki) and a black ball are mentioned therein.

[30] Fernandez merely observes that there were many people in good array.

[31] The Chiquitos observed by Nordenskiöld also danced as they played.

[32] Iraisòs specifies that head and shoulder were used to strike the ball, but Fernandez and Nordenskiöld agree with d'Oribigny in mentioning only the use of the head. The latter two also comment upon the reckless manner in which players dived to recover the low balls.

[33] d'Orbigny, 1835—47, vol. 2, p. 86.

[34] Nordenskiöld, 1922, p. 28.

[35] Nordenskiöld, 1920, p. 101f. In footnote 1, p. 101, this writer quotes from p. 409 of the Litterae Annua for 1605 a passage which he states refers to the Chané: "'Indos videlicet huius Prouinciae, pilae ludo capitibus tabellarum loco, tanta dexteritate exerceri, quanta Hispani, manibus, atque tabellis.'"

Chiriguano (Tupi-Guaraní linguistic stock)[36]

The author states that he has heard of a game called *bondi* among the Chiriguano. It is played with a solid rubber ball, using only the head. The ball must not be touched with the hands, nor must it be allowed to touch the ground.

Dr. Métraux informs me[37] that Baron Nordenskiöld's informant was a Chané, and that this bit of hearsay was never confirmed. The Chiriguano occurrence must thus be set aside; it is omitted from further consideration here. It is suggested that the Chané informant referred to his own game, or that of the Chiquito. The only variant detail is the native term, for which I have been unable to discover a Chiquitoan cognate. Possibly it is Arawakan, in which case a possible Tainan equivalent is suggested in the word, *batey*, for which an identical meaning exists.

Itatin: modern Guarayù (Tupi-Guaraní linguistic stock)[38]

The ball, made from the resin of a tree, is solid, yet light, and at the slightest touch it bounces better than the inflated ball of Europe. Moreover, it is not struck with hand or foot, but with the head and, if need be, with the elbow, sending and receiving with wondrous skill. A great prize is given to the victor.

Other Southern Guaraní Peoples[39]

Evidence on the ball game among the southern and southeastern Guaraní is not definitive. It is known that the Itatin arrived in relatively late times from Paraguay. Dr. Métraux has, indeed, recently informed me, in the course of conversation, that he believes the passage from Peramas quoted below refers to that tribe. It must be admitted that

[36] Ibid, p. 104.

[37] In conversation, 1947.

[38] Nordenskiöld, 1920, p. 102, fn 3: quotation from the Litterae Annuae of 1589, p. 434, as follows: "'Pila est e cuiusdam resina arboris compacta, leuis tamen, et quæ minimo pulsu magis resiliat, quam folliculus quicumque: eam porro non manu impellunt, aut pede, fed [*sic*] capite, et, si forte, cubito, mira dantium accipientiumque dexteritate: et est magnum victori praemium'".

[39] Métraux, 1928, p. 213, note 1, quotes a pertinent sentence from Joseph Emmanuel Peramas, *De vita et moribus tredecim virorum paraguaycorum*. Faventiae, 1793. P. 57: "'Pilam autem Guaranii non (ut nos) manu, sed superiore parte nudi pedis mittunt remittuntque, idque expeditissime, ac dexterrime.'"

Iraisòs, quoted by Gilij (vol. 2, bk. 4, Note, p. 387): "Ho anche inteso da un ex-missionario del *Paraguai*, che i *Guaranesi* ... tra' quali è molto usata codella palla, si servono per risospingerla, di piedi, e gambe, e ginocchi, appunto come i *Mossi*..."

neither of the two brief statements given below resolve themselves very well with that from the Litterae Annuae. They specify the use of foot and other parts of the body, but not the head, while the Litterae explicitly state that head, and not foot, was used. These are minor items, to be sure: one author may well omit what another stressed. Nevertheless the divergency is sufficiently great to prevent application for the present of the Peramas and Iraisòs statements to the Itatin.

Further evidence that the Guaraní proper knew a rubber-ball game is to be found in the *Arte, vocabulario y tesoro de la lengua Tupi ó Guaraní* of Montoya. Since most of Montoya's work was done among the Guaraní of El Guaira, just east of the Paraná River, between the Tieté and Iguassú Rivers[40] it seems probable that his vocabulary also came from the same general region. The pertinent words are:

"Mangaí, *Arbol que dá las pelotas que llaman de nervios*...
Mangaicĭ, *la resina de que hazen las pelotas*... *Pelota para jugar, Mãngá.*"

The *manga* tree is no doubt the *mangaba* of Martius,[41] which is to say the *Mangabeira (Hancornia speciosa)* of that region.

It must be evident from the foregoing that at least some of the southern Guaraní did possess a rubber-ball game. The strongest probability is that it reached them from the Mojos-Chiquitos area. We need not postulate a slow diffusion, for it could easily have been obtained in the course of the numerous westward migrations of Guaraní elements.

To the north and northeast of the Mojos-Chiquitos area lie four tribes manifesting games that bear strong resemblances to those of the Paressí, Mojo, and Chiquito. These are the Amniapä, Hauri, Kepikiriwat, and Nambikuàra, accounts of which follow.

Amniapä (Tupi-Guaraní linguistic family)[42]

Ball: The ball is hollow and of the size of a man's fist (ca. 4 inches in diameter ?).

Court: The game is held in the central plaza, on the clean, bare surface of which the court is laid out. At each side, a pair of palm-leaf petioles, stripped of leaves, is planted. A line appears in the photographs, traced in the surface of the court, running across the court from one pair of markers to the other. It appears to constitute the center line, dividing the court into two halves. No boundary lines are either depicted or mentioned in the text.

Players: Adult men alone participate in the game, with the women forming an appreciative audience. When the men are tired, the children

[40] Métraux, 1948, p. 78.
[41] Vol. 2, p. 400.
[42] Snethlage, 1937, pp. 105, 108, 109 and plates 26 and 27.

take over and imitate them; but since they are less adept, their game shortly becomes a sort of football.

Teams comprise three players on each side: the community itself appears to be small. Participants appear only in breechclout and leg- and arm-bands, which seems to be the usual garb.

Wagers, markers, etc.: Each player lays a wager of two arrows, the collected stakes being piled at one side of the court near the center. On each side of the court six kernels of maize are laid in a line. They serve to keep the score during the game.

Snethlage describes games both within a community and between the men of two neighboring villages. He makes no mention of referees or other officials in either case.

Play: Players are shown awaiting the ball in a line across the court at some depth from the center, but once the game has started, it is evident that they no longer play in position. Only the head may strike the ball; players dive to the ground to retrieve a shot that rolls along the ground and return it with the head. It is a body fault to touch the ball with any other part of the body and counts a point against the offending player. Should the ball, in rolling, fail to pass the center line, a point is again scored against the offending team. For each point thus scored, the gaining team received a maize kernel. Finally, all of the score markers have passed to the side of one team, and it only remains for another point to be scored by the leading side. If their rivals win that play instead, they get two points. The victors win the six arrows (two per losing player) of the vanquished. In all probability, the stakes are equally divided.

After an inter-community game, there is a feast of chicha, peanuts, and bananas. In the instance described by Snethlage, it was the home team that lost; and it was they that feasted their visitors.

No religious or magical concommitants were noted.

Huari (Unaffiliated)[43]

"I saw the small tribe of Huari Indians near the Upper Rio Guaporé playing the hollow india-rubber ball game. There also the balls had to be caught and butted with the head." A specimen ball is described as being about six cm. (between two and three inches) in diameter, with a wall thickness of about six to seven milimeters.

Kepikiriwat (Tupi-Guarani linguistic stock?)[44]

Ceremonial ball games are played between moieties. The ball is struck with the head. Arrows form the stakes.

[43] Nordenskiöld, 1920, p. 104.
[44] Lévi-Strauss, 1948, p. 375.

Since the game was not observed, but had to be reported on the basis of information from the natives,[45] no further information is at present available.

Nambikuára (Unaffiliated)

In 1942, the Reverend Willard R. Elton, of Berwyn, Pennsylvania, while engaged in missionary activity in Matto Grosso under the auspices of the South American Indian Mission, witnessed a ball game among the Nambikuára; and it is through his kindness that I am able to present the following particulars.[46]

The game was observed at a village on the Rio Duvida, some fifteen or twenty miles south of José Bonifacio. Here a population of approximately 150 inhabitants, said to be the remnant of three tribes,[47] lives in twelve houses bordering a roughly rectangular central plaza.

The Elton party upon arrival was lodged in the chief's house, a rectangular structure located at a corner of the shorter side of the plaza. In the late afternoon, at approximately four o'clock, the chief arranged an exhibition match for the visitors. This he did simply by speaking to the men and designating the participants. All were young men – Mr. Elton estimates their ages to have been between 16 and 23 years – and all wore only the habitual gee-string. Since the walls of the houses were open, women at their household tasks could freely observe the game, which took place in the central plaza.

The plaza, measuring some fifteen by thirty yards, was clear and level though encroaching grass had not been eradicated. No boundary or dividing lines were drawn, and no markers placed; nor does play, which was directed down the length of the court, appear to have had reference to any such limits.

The players that had been selected, five men on each side, trotted out to the far ends of the plaza, where they took up positions in a line across

---

[45] Claude Lévi-Strauss, Letter, dated, April 28, 1947.

[46] Although the Reverend Elton gave an oral account from memory, his recollection of details was exceptionally clear, no doubt owing in part to the fact that he has delivered lectures on his experiences. Three photographs of the game in progress served to refresh his memory and amplified his description.

[47] Unfortunately, the Rev. Elton was unable to recall the names of these tribes. The villagers called themselves "Sabones", possibly to be equated with Sabanê, the name of a Nambikuára group (Métraux, 1942, note 23.) On the other hand, they appeared to be able to converse with some difficulty with the "Aritiua," said to be a Nambikuára sub-group but more probably to be equated with the Paressí (Ariti). Indeed, influences are probably Paressí. Only in the absence of hammocks (the villagers sleep on the ground) do the gross arrangements of the "Sabones" resemble those of the Nambikuára.

If the above interpretation is correct, there are grounds for assuming that the rubber-ball game is a recent introduction from the Paressí into this community.

the court. Meanwhile, the chief had gone inside his house, to rummage among the Elton's effects for gift knives he had previously noticed. Having found about a dozen of them – and reassuring the visitors as to his intentions – he returned to the plaza and took up a position on the sidelines, at the middle of the court, where he laid the knives in a row before him.

The game began when a player threw the ball to the opposing side in an underhand serve that barely cleared the ground. All players might be standing; or, as a photograph shows, one member of each team might be on hands and knees at the serve. Whichever method was employed, and the second requires further clarification, the man nearest to whom the ball fell returned it. This he did by diving to the ground, hands beneath his chest to take the shock, while with a vigorous toss of his head he sent the ball flying back. A shot that rolled along the ground was still valid. Aside from the serve, the ball was touched only with the head. High drives were recovered by a player leaping into the air, as in soccer. Teammates might strike the ball in succession. As play progressed, the participants became a confused mass of bodies in the center of the court, although there was no invasion of the opponents' court.

The method of scoring is obscure. Nothing corresponding to a body fault was recalled by Mr. Elton, nor did there appear to be goals of any sort. Indeed, all that he and his party could agree upon, when reviewing what they had seen, was that from the shouting players a cry would go up when the ball rose to an extreme height. The play was suspended while the scoring player made his way to the knives, about which he danced in stiff-legged manner three or more times, hooting as he danced. When he had done, he picked out a knife and stuck it through his gee-string behind him, after which he made his way back to his place and the game was resumed. Thus the game went on, to the accompaniment of what seemed to be taunts exchanged between the teams. At the end of about an hour, the weary men by common accord put an end to the game and gathered about the chief and the White spectators. A lively, yet amicable postmortem discussion sprang up, as the players compared the number of knives they had won. These markers, which might as well have functioned as stakes or a prize, were then turned in to the chief, who gave them back to the Eltons. Later, the knives were presented to the chief. The final disposition of them among the tribesmen seems to have had nothing to do with the game.

While the men were still talking at the side of the court, the younger boys had sallied forth, formed their teams, and launched into a vigorous imitation of their elders.

Little can be said as to the associations of the game. While competitive, it struck the Rev. Elton as being purely recreational in nature; and the dance about the knives was in his view merely a dance of triumph.

The ball itself was made from the latex of the *Syringea (Hevea)* tree, which was gathered by the men. A clay core, from which a hollow grass stem projected, was covered with successive coats of latex until a wall of the desired thickness had been built up. Water was then dropped down the hollow stem to dissolve the clay core, and the solution was shaken out. When only a hollow ball remained, the straw was removed and the hole plugged with latex. The finished article was about the size of an indoor baseball (i. e. about four in. in diameter), and seems to have been highly valued, since the Eltons tried in vain to barter for a specimen.

Auetö (Tupi-Guaraní linguistic stock)[48]

"Rubber balls, yet solid, occurred among the Auetö. The sap of a *Figueira* or the mangave is rolled into a little ball on the chest, is steeped in ash-water and the ball is pricked all around in such a manner that the exterior appears to be covered with weaving. The balls are stained red with urucú."

The first stage of manufacture recalls strongly that described for the Chiquitos (see above).

Apinayé (Ge linguistic stock)[49]

Among the Apinayé, the rubber-ball game is bound up, part and parcel, with the young men's initiation ceremonies, of which it occupies a phase. By the time they enter upon the *peny-ta'g* ceremony, as it is known, the candidates have already achieved the status of warriors. Since the present concern is with the components characteristic to the game itself, many ritual features which appear directly dependent upon the special nature of the ceremony have either been simplified or omitted.

The ball *(peny-krā)* is made especially for the ceremony. A group of candidates issue forth from the village with gourd bowls, in which they collect the latex that issues from slashes made in the bark of the *mangabeira* tree *(Hancornia speciosa*; Apinayé: *peny)*. Back at the village, the latex is smeared in broad strips upon the bodies of candidates, repeated applications building up the thickness. Meanwhile, other members of the class have prepared clay cores. When the latex bands are ready, they are rolled off the body onto the moulds until the desired shell has been attained. The core is then broken up and the fragments extracted through a slit made in the rubber. Finally, additional strips are added to cover the slit and complete the construction of the hollow ball.

---

[48] von den Steinen, p. 329 (my translation).
[49] Nimuendajú, 1939, pp. 61—7.

For the game which Nimuendajú observed, six small balls *(peny-krā-ñgri're)* about 5 cm. (2 inches) in diameter were made and four larger ones *(ambl'dv)* with tails of bunched ostrich feathers, as well as one large ball *(peny-krā-maati')* with seeds inside like a rattle. The second type of ball suggests a shuttlecock; and it may be because of this that its name does not share the **peny-krā* element with the other types.

Yet another feature in which the game suggests the shuttlecock and maize-leaf ball games, is in the use of wooden battledores *(pali-re)*. For ordinary players these take the form of short-handled rectulangular paddles with an overall length of approximately 30 cm. (12 inches). For the ceremonial moiety directors, on the other hand, the battledore is a hollow log, some 40 cm. (16 inches) in length, into which the player thrusts his arm and grasps as handhold a transverse stick set within. Both types of battledore bear painted designs.

The candidates themselves do not participate in the game, which they may not even witness. The players comprise the mature men *(uyapē')*, who are divided according to moiety into two teams, each led by a ceremonial director. How many players are involved is not stated, although Nimuendajú's diagram depicts a director· and four players on each side. A counselor, who is also shown, occupies a position which may roughly be equated with that of umpire among other tribes.

On the evening before the game, the *uyapē'* dress as for a log-race and dance with clubs in the central plaza. About the plaza there runs a concentric boulevard, upon which the houses of the village front. Radial paths at the cardinal points connect the plaza with the boulevard. During the dance, the counselor, unseen by the *uyapē'*, makes a counter-clockwise circuit of the boulevard, bearing the large rubber ball.

Early the next morning, the players dance again in the plaza, until at daybreak the counselor comes forth with the large ball. The teams then take up positions upon the eastern radial path, forming two opposed rows. The counselor then hands the ball to the director of one team, who passes it to his counterpart on the rival side; and thus it travels from hand to hand until it has made the rounds of the players and is returned to the elder. Now it is thrown to the first director, who strikes it smartly into the air. His opponent receives it as it falls and sends it aloft again, after which it is allowed to fall to the ground.

One of the small balls is now tossed between the waiting teams, and the game moves to the plaza, where it continues. A little later, the shuttlecock-like ball replaces the small one. At noon, the ceremony with the large ball is repeated, the opposite director being first to receive it.

In the afternoon, the teams withdraw once more to the eastern path, where they stand facing each other as before. There, a man accompanying the director of one moiety makes a menacing feint with the large ball toward the rival team, then rolls it before their feet, Their director picks it up, strikes it aloft once, and thus terminates the *peny-ta'g* ceremony.

"True to their frequent practice," observes Nimuendajú, "the Apinayé connect the origin of *peny-ta'g* with a tale that originally has nothing to do with rubber-balls; nor is there any bond between its two constituent episodes. (p. 64).... It is obvious that these extraordinarily solemn and impressive ceremonies have no basic connection with the Sharpened Leg and Rolling Skull tales. On the other hand, it is conceivable that they sprang from the Apinayé Sun cult, though the memory of such an association has completely vanished from these Indians' consciousness" (p. 67).

It does not seem amiss to anticipate at this juncture the more general evaluation which concludes this paper, in summarizing the unusual character of the Apinayé game. Details of play and of scoring are unfortunately too scanty to permit extended comparison. Nonetheless, the ceremony within the confined limits of the eastern path suggests that the ball is struck upward, rather than toward the other team. Whether this is also true of the game in the plaza cannot be ascertained. Striking the ball aloft, together with the use of battledore and shuttlecock, are all features of the maize-leaf ball game, a form of which occurs among the Apinayé men themselves.[50] It is indeed possible that the *peny-ta'g* game has closer historical connection with the circle games of Sherente (see below), Macusi, Mojos, etc. There is little doubt that, to the tribe as to the ethnographer, primary interest among the Apinayé centered upon the ceremonial aspects of *peny-ta'g*. In a moiety-organized society ceremonial emphasis may well give rise to team play and to the role of the counselor which we have noted. The precedent of the log race, already before their eyes, might have been another factor in the transformation of the circle game into the competitive game just described.

These considerations arise from the geographically isolated position of the Apinayé game with respect to other competitive rubber-ball games, as well as from the unique characteristics it presents. That the changes outlined above actually occurred cannot be demonstrated; but their possibility invites caution in the establishment of historical relationships.

Sherente (Ge linguistic stock)

Only one clan, the *prase'*, of the eight that comprised the Sherente possessed the right to play the ball game. The *prase'* comprised the remnants of a tribe known as the Sampe', from the headwaters of the Rio Bananal. From the game *(klito')* they received an alternate designation, *klito'-tedekwa'*.[51]

---

[50] Snethlage, 1931, p. 182; Nimuendajú, 1939, pp. 97, 117.
[51] Nimuendajú, 1942, p. 19.

...The balls (*klito'*, also applied to a coronal tonsure) are 5 cm. in diameter, somewhat flattened, and consist of a core of dry steppe grass covered by many thin layers of mangabeira rubber. The elders, who manufacture the ball, smear the sap in stripes on their abdomens, allowing it to congeal, and wrap these thin rubber skins round the core. Attached to the ball is a cluster of arara tail feathers loosely dangling from short chains of beads. The ball is brought to the assembled players on a large gourd bowl painted red. They form a circle and, undivided into teams, throw the ball at one another with the palm of the hand. The wrist is wrapped with bark.

At this amusement the other clans are at best represented by a few boys. There is no special occasion for arranging a game; it is played whenever the spirit moves the members. Other clans play ball by the same method, but invariably with balls of maize husks[52].

Galibi (Cariban linguistic stock)

Balls, syringe bulbs, and rings are made from the milk which flows from a liana belonging to the *Apocyna*. The latex is boiled, then poured over prepared clay forms or within clay moulds. The entire apparatus is then dried over the fire, which blackens the rubber. Finally the moulds are broken and the finished object emerges. The ball, judging by this description, is in all probability hollow. There is no information as to the game in which it was used.[53]

Macusi and Patamona (Cariban linguistic stock)

I have also seen Makusi and Patamona boys playing with a rubber ball on the following lines: With the boys standing around in a circle ... and keeping their relative positions in it throughout the game, the ball is thrown into the air and before reaching the ground must be struck by the flat of the hand. With this increased impetus it strikes the ground with greater force and a correspondingly greater rebound, when it is again struck while falling in similar fashion, and the game is to see how many times running a player can strike the ball on the fall. As soon as one boy misses his stroke, another has a try, and so on. It is no mean feat to keep the ball rebounding but half a dozen times on a rough, uneven surface.[54]

Im Thurn notes that among the Macusi the rubber ball is used in place of one made of "part of an ear of Indian corn,"[55] and a comparison of Roth's account given above with Schomburgk's description of the maize-leaf ball game of that tribe[56] offers convincing proof that the two games are in essence one and the same.

---

[52] Ibid, pp. 22—3.

[53] Barrère, pp. 139—141, plate facing p. 139. I am indebted to Dr. Alfred Métraux for the ascription of Barrère's account to the Galibi.

[54] Roth, p. 490 pl. 172 c.

[55] Im Thurn, p. 326.

[56] Vol. 2, p. 151.

Akawai (Cariban linguistic stock)

The Indians prepare for their games great balls of this elastic gum, ...; they call the *Siphonia elastica* "*hatti*," the rubber-yielding Ficoids, like the gum, "*Cuinac*" ... The Indian women gather the milk, which trickles freely from uts made in the trunk, in bags twisted from banana leaves, and then sprea it with their fingers in thin layers on their bare legs, whereby it immedie ely assumes a horny, viscous consistency. These layers they roll together with the palms of the hands and twist them into spheres, whereupon they again prepare new layers and with them wrap around the ball that has already been prepared until it has attained the desired circumference. The color of the same, indeed through the action of the air alone, becomes black, and it hardens very quickly; I have never seen it hung over the smoke for this purpose, since the heat would make it sticky.[57]

Tamanac (Cariban linguistic stock)

The Tamanac have no rubber-ball game. Lovén erroneously credits them with the rubber ball, but the pertinent passage in Gilij, which he cites, actually refers to the maize-leaf ball.[58]

[57] Appun, vol. 2, pp. 153f (my translation).
[58] Lovén, p. 526. Cf. Gilij, vol. 2, p. 269; "Noi incominceremo le nostre osservazione dalla qualita della palla; la quale non è, come le nostre, ripiena di cimatura; o come quella de' *Tamanàchi*, formata con foglie di granturco tra sè congegnate...."

CHAPTER THREE

THE GAMES IN THE ANTILLES AND CENTRAL AMERICA

Taino and Lucayans (Arawakan linguistic stock)

It was in the Antilles, on the island of Haiti, that the Spaniards had their first glimpse of the game which they were thereafter to know as *batey*. Subsequently, it was observed in Puerto Rico, and it may have been present in the Bahamas as well.[1]

Game: the game itself, together with the ball and the court in which it took place, all bore the name, *batéy* (or *bateo*) "la letra *e* luenga," as Las Casas carefully points out.[2]

---

[1] *Haiti:* Our two best sources are Oviedo (vol. 1, bk. 5, chs. 1, p. 163, and 2, pp. 165—7) and Las Casas (1909, chs. 46, p. 121, and 204, p. 538; 1877, bk. 2, ch. 9, p. 29). The latter appears to have been followed in part by Torquemada (vol. 1, bk. 3, ch. 3, p. 247f.) whose remarks are, however, applied in general to Haiti, Cuba, Puerto Rico, Jamaica, and the Bahamas. Herrera likewise makes a purely derivative remark concerning Haiti (dec. 1, bk. 6, ch. 4, p. 152; dec. 1, bk. 3, ch. 4, p. 70). Charlevoix (vol. 1, pp. 52—3), while presenting some independent data, refers for much of his material to Oviedo.

Puerto Rico: Oviedo (vol. 1, bk. 16, chs. 4, p. 471, 5, p. 472, and 16, p. 488), is the chief authority. Cf. also Torquemada, loc. cit., and Herrera (dec. 1, bk. 8, ch. 12, p. 224).

Bahamas: Martyr (dec. 7, bk. 1, ch. 2, p. 502; bk. 2, ch. 3, p. 508) refers twice to the "juego de pelota" of the islanders, in the second instance alluding to the dexterity which they exhibited in play. Admittedly, the evidence is only inferential with reference to the type of game played. Torquemada's remarks *(loc. cit.)* may offer a measure of corroboration, if they are not in turn based upon Martyr.

Virgin Islands: The only evidence for this group lies in archeological finds, interpreted as ball courts by Hatt (p. 38).

In the description of the Haitian game, the initials of the author will be appended to the passages for which he is the source: thus, Las Casas (LC), Oviedo (O), and Charlevoix (C).

[2] 1909, ch. 204, p. 538. Schuller finds (p. 113) an etymological cognate in Arawakan *at, ata, ada,* wood, tree. The word has an interesting history subsequent to the conquest of the mainland. There it was occasionally applied to the Mexican game: we find Tezozomoc himself, full-bred descendent of Mexican royalty, using it in the form, *batel* (p. 227). As we shall see, the word in its Antillean form is given as the local native term for the court among the Acaxee of Sinaloa and Durango (Santarén, quoted in Alegre, vol. 1, bk. 4, pp. 405—7; cited by Ribas, bk. 8, ch. 3, p. 476), as well as among the Yaqui of the Sinaloa coast (Ribas, bk. 1, ch. 4, p. 15). In more recent times, the Yaqui have called the sticks used in the stick race, *kuta bateyim teyeunaki,* which Beals relates to this term (1943, p. 44). Orozco y Berra, Tezozomoc's editor (p. 227, note 2), points out that the word is currently applied in Cuba to the area or space occupied by structures or to the patio or plaza of rural haciendas.

Blom's suggested comparison of the Antillean term with Quiché Maya *bate* must be deferred for the present.

Ball: The latex that flowed from cuts made in the bark of a certain tree growing in Haiti (LC), together with plants and juices and "a mixture of things" (O), was cooked until it formed a paste, which the islanders rounded into a ball, shaping it with a stone (LC). The finished product, of about the size of the inflated ball used in certain European games,[3] was heavy, yet of a spongy texture. The rubber by this time had turned black and no longer stuck to the hands. The resiliency of the balls was always a source of wonder to the Spaniards, who regularly comment upon it.

Courts: The Haitian settlement pattern was simple. The houses clustered about a central plaza, upon which the house of the chief fronted. Within the plaza the principal ball court (batéy) was located. In addition, larger towns had other, ancillary, courts of lesser size (LC).[4] Las Casas describes the principal court as being level, clean-swept, and rectangular in plan, with a length three times the width. Low mounds one or two spans (8 to 16 inches) in height surrounded it. Oviedo adds that spectators sat on stones about the court, while the chiefs made use of their wooden stools (duhos). Archeological excavations have shown that the stones were incorporated in the mounds themselves. It is probable, to judge from the statements of Oviedo, that the courts on the outskirts of town were generally similar in character.

During play, the court was divided in half by a line (O)(C), possibly longitudinally, though there are grounds for belief that the dividing line lay along the smaller axis of the court.[5]

There is no evidence as to the ownership of the court: in all probability it was community property.

Players: As among the Otomac, both men and women participated in the game; teams might comprise only one sex; married women might play against maidens, or maidens against youths (O). Las Casas affirms that women played only against their own sex. At any rate, a mixed team is unreported. When playing, men wore a loin cloth as large as a hand in size, while chiefs' wives and the principal women donned a short apron, reaching only to the knees, when they played ball (O).

Teams: Large numbers of players took part in each game. Oviedo states that there were ten to twenty, Las Casas twenty to thirty, persons

[3] While these games will be treated in more detail below, it may be noted here that a diameter roughly 4—6 inches is indicated, judging from old prints and descriptions.

[4] The latter may be identified in part with the courts mentioned by Oviedo as being situated at the exits of the town, although he claimed that they were larger than the central courts. Charlevoix adds that the larger, peripheral courts served to receive larger groups, as in intercommunity matches.

[5] The statement of Las Casas (1909, p. 538), which permits of either interpretation, runs, "Poníanse veinte y treinta de cada parte á la luenga de la plaza..."

on a side. Teams were equal in number. Play was continual, and the court is said to have been in constant use (O).

Wagers were ventured, not only by the players themselves, but also, in inter-village games, by their caciques. Las Casas mentions one such game between two communities in which one cacique ᴐet a scarlet shirt against an old ornamental covering (un paño viejo de tocar), a value, he adds, the equivalent of one hundred castellanos.

Play: Oviedo states merely that the ball might be struck with shoulder, elbow, head, knee, and more frequently with the hip; while Charlevoix observes that head, hips, elbows, and the knees above all were used. On the other hand, Las Casas is more specific, stating that men took high balls with the shoulder, low ones with the hip, while women commonly used their knees or closed fists. Such differences of play along sex lines are again strongly reminiscent of the Otomac. Great agility characterized the play, participants leaping into the air to return a high volley and diving to the earth, bracing the body with the right hand to throw the hip against a ground-grazing ball.

When a game began, the teams took their places on the court, which was divided by a line between them which no player might cross (O, C). Since Las Casas states that the members of each team took their place along the length of the plaza, it has been suggested with reason[6] that the teams must have been drawn up facing each other along the major axis of the court. Without denying the validity of this interpretation, I feel that another is likewise tenable, namely that the two teams faced each other across the minor (transverse) axis, while the individuals comprising each side strung out in depth down the length of the court.

The ball was put into play by one of the participants, who threw or struck it to the opposing team. The player nearest to whom it landed returned it. A ball was good as long as it bounced and was within bounds, but when it skimmed the ground or rolled it went dead (O). "And the object of the game," Oviedo tells us, "is that those of this side make it pass beyond the area before their opponents or the latter send it out of bounds or outside the court of the former..." (p. 165). Play continued until one side or the other lost the ball by letting it pass their goal or permitting it to die in their court.[7] A ball that went out of bounds was

---

[6] Lovén, pp. 94, 95, 524.

[7] Lovén states that the game must have been played against the long walls of the court, especially since the Puerto Rican plazas excavated by Mason (1941, *passim*) possess only side walls. While there is little doubt that the ball must have gone dead when it passed beyond the side walls, it is not easy to construe them as goals. For one thing, the dimensions given by Mason (ranging from 62' × 27' to 200' × 55') would in many cases make it comparatively easy, in a game played across the court, to send the ball over the low side walls. It must be borne in mind that under these circumstances a player would have to send

returned to the side that had put it into play for a new serve. A goal or dead ball scored a point, the total number to be won being agreed upon beforehand by both parties. The two teams alternated in service (O).

As described by the early writers, the game of *batey* appears to have been exclusively secular. It is, of course, true that the courts also formed the scene of community festivals and dances, some of which seem to have partaken of a religious character. Nonetheless, the dual function of the ball courts may safely be viewed as an index of their focal position with regard to the community in both its material and social mani-festations.[8] "When the cacicazco was strongly developed, as in Espa-nola," observes Lovén (p. 338), "the plaza was used for the represen-tative communication between the cacique and the people."

While extensive discussion of archeological data would be out of place here, it may not be amiss to stress certain conclusions relating to chrono-logy which have been reached by recent archeologists. There is general agreement that recognizable plazas of the ball-court type are confined to the western portions of the Virgin Islands, to Puerto Rico, Haiti, and to the adjacent tip of Cuba.[9] Rouse considers them characteristic of "Taino" culture and in effect places them in his most recent (period IV) horizon.[10] This does not, however, rule out the possibility that the game may have been present from an earlier time, in conjunction with a non-structural court of the type encountered within the tropical forests of South America.

the ball much less than the total width of the court, sometimes only half that distance. It will be seen that scoring would follow almost every play.

The ranges stated to have been achieved by players elsewhere in the Americas under comparable conditions buttress this belief. In addition, it is probable that the side walls held the spectators, who might be expected to have interfered with such play. It seems indicated that the goals were at the ends of the court.

Finally, it is no longer entirely correct to assert that the Puerto Rican plazas possessed only side walls, for Mason (*op. cit.*, p. 247) is specific in describing low terminal walls for two plazas (B, E) at Capá, Utuado.

[8] At the time of the uprising of 1511, when the Indians of Puerto Rico revolted against their White *encomenderos*, a local chieftain seized a Spanish youth and ordered the members of his household to play ball for him, the victors being privileged to slay him. The game took place in the afternoon; but before it ended a Spaniard, warned by a loyal Indian, arrived and put the villagers to flight. It is suggestive that this episode finds the ball game, as sportive play, transformed into a cat-and-mouse relationship, with the life of the captive as wager (Herrera, dec. 1, bk. 8, ch. 12, p. 224; see also Oviedo, bk. 16, ch. 5. p. 488).

[9] Some sources may be cited, without attempting to exhaust their number. Fewkes (pp. 79—85) gives general information for the Antilles; Hatt (p. 38) for the Virgin Islands; Stahl, (pp. 181—5), Mason, (1941, pp. 247—254, 262—3, Figs. 2, 4, and 5), and Rainey (pp. 98, 101f) for Puerto Rico; and Harrington *(passim)* for Cuba.

[10] Rouse, p. 145 and Table 7.

Circum-Caribbean Mainland

As previously noted, the Otomac are properly subsumed among the tribes of the circum-Caribbean mainland,[11] and it is probable, though not at present subject to proof, that in many ways the Otomac ball game resembled cognate games among the peoples of Central America. Evidence for the occurrence of the rubber-ball game in the latter region, while scant and sporadic, does show it to have been present there. Speaking of the customs of the natives of the province of Darien, Gómara alludes to ball games. Oviedo is more specific: he states that the game of *batey* played by the Indians of Cueva (the present Cordillera de San Blas, Panama) was sufficiently covered by his description of the game in Haiti. Finally, the licentiate Espinosa reported of his first *entrada* that the cacique Tabraba, whose kingdom lay in the sierra inland from the Azuero Peninsula, was the first chieftain met in those parts who played *batey*.[12] The route followed by Espinosa led out from Antigua, turning south before he reached the Cueva region, then proceeding westward parallel to the southern coastline. The game may thus be considered to have been rare in those regions, though not necessarily absent, since the Spaniards did not often have a chance to witness the peaceful pursuits of the natives they visited. Taken together with Gómara's statement, the testimony of Oviedo and Espinosa suggest that it was played in the highlands of Panama. On the other hand, too much significance must not be attached to their comparisons with the Antillean game, for Oviedo and Espinosa had not witnessed the Mexican cognate, and so could only describe what they had seen by reference to Haiti.

Between Panama and El Salvador, where the southernmost archeological evidence for the ball game occurs, there lies a large region for which there is only meagre information. Lovén thrice refers to a "ball from the Mosquito Coast" in the Gothenburg Museum, which he describes as "massive, very hard and covered with strips of palm leaves, the same as a hollow rubber ball from the Cavinas." In the Museum, he adds, "there is also a piece of the sticky mass full of shreds and fibers

[11] See Kirchoff, 1948, p. 439.

[12] Lothrop (1937, p. 27) cites all three sources. The original passages run as follows:

Gómara, 1877, p. 199: Costumbres de los del Darien: "Los bailes que usan son areitos, y los juegos pelota."

Oviedo, vol. 3, bk. 29, ch. 32, p. 159: De algunas particularidades de los indios de Cueva...: "En la primera parte desta *General historia,* en el libro VI [treating with Haiti, etc.] se tractó de diversas cosas, assi como de las moradas de los indios; y en esta materia en esta libro XXIX se dixeron otras cosas diferençiadas.

"En el juego del batey y en los huracanes basta lo dicho y escripto."

Espinosa, p. 510: (of Tabraba) "Este es el primero cacique que en estas partes se ha hallado el juego del *bateyn* que se usa en Haity."

of which the Mosquito balls are made."[13] The value of this ball as evidence is somewhat augmented by the description which Conzemius gives of the gathering of rubber by the Miskito and Sumu Indians. While the commercial exploitation of the native *Castilla* tree began about 1860, rubber had been gathered prior to that date. Furthermore, the use of the sap of a vine *(Ipomoea bona-nox)* or from a liana *(Calonyction speciosum)* to coagulate the latex is reminiscent of similar aboriginal practice elsewhere.[14] However Conzemius mentions neither rubber balls nor, in fact, any ball games whatsoever among these peoples.

In Honduras, the site of Tenampua, ascribed to the Lenca, contains a ball court which presents detailed similarities to those of the Maya to the west. The resemblances are such as to refer the court to Maya stimuli in the opinion of several investigators;[15] and it would be hazardous, therefore, to consider it representative of the playing fields in which the Central American versions of the game took place.

The courts of El Salvador likewise appear to reflect Maya types rather than those that may have existed farther to the south.

Maya (Mayan linguistic stock)

Rich in the archeological testimony of ball courts, the Maya area paradoxically lacks a single extensive account that can be said specifically to describe the game played there. Two of the early chroniclers of New Spain were, it is true, in a position to observe it among the late Maya;[16] but since neither worked exclusively among the Maya it would be unwise to refer their accounts solely to that people. Moreover, by the time they made their observations the Maya game had already been subjected to profound influences from the Mexican regions; "Toltec" and

[13] Lovén, p. 525 (both quotations); see also p. 679f.

A request for further details directed to the Gothenburg Ethnographic Museum elicited the following information from Mr. Karl-Erik Larsson, of that institution (Letter, dated July 15th, 1947): The ball in question was collected by Mr. Otto A. F. Braütigam, of Göteborg, and presented to the Museum in 1931. He had found it on one of his plantations on the Rio Cooringwas. A sketch which accompanies the letter indicates that the specimen is somewhat flattened, perhaps through storage, and that its diameters accordingly vary between 5 and 6 centimeters.

[14] Conzemius, p. 46f.

[15] See especially Yde, p. 22f., citing Popenoe. The court has been described and depicted by Squier (1858, p. 127f.; 1869), Lothrop (1927, p. 25, pl. III), Popenoe (pp. 566, 568), and Yde (pp. 20—3, fig. 5).

[16] Motolinia (Toribio de Benavente), a member of the first priestly delegation to be sent to New Spain (1524), subsequently served in central Mexico, in Guatemala and Nicaragua, then in Puebla, in the Tehuantepec region, and finally in Tlaxcala. Durán, according to Joyce (1933, p. xxii), also had an opportunity to witness the Maya game.

"Nahuatl" are terms which indicate some of the vehicles of the influence which had modified the court and possibly the game as well.

Evidence for the earlier form of the Maya game must accordingly be gleaned from the known ball courts and from archeological representations of players. To this may be added the pertinent references in the Quiché Maya chronicle, the Popol Vuh. Of the latter, it must be borne in mind that the original document is post-Conquest in time, and thus the antiquity of the account in its present form cannot be ascertained. Consequently, the information it offers cannot be used to determine the state of the Maya game prior to the period of Mexican influence. Its value lies chiefly in its position as the sole account known specifically to apply to the Maya.[17]

Still another proviso must be made. The ball courts thus far excavated show both regional and temporal differences in structure. Some of these disparities no doubt reflect merely architectural variations, but others may have gone hand in hand with deviant forms of play. Of this we have only the faintest inkling today. The Popol Vuh, as I have said, refers to the game played at some unspecified period by the Quiché Maya, and it is only by inference that it can be extended to cover the games played by other peoples in the Maya area.

The linguistic terms in the description to follow are those contained in the Popol Vuh. A more extensive comparison with cognates from other dialects will be found at the end of this section.

Game: The rubber-ball game was known by the term *chaah* (p. 71).

Ball: The word, *quiq*, blood, sap, by which the ball was designated appears to refer to the latex from which it was made. While there is no information as to its weight or to the method by which it was manufactured, its size is suggested by bas-reliefs and figurines as being half that of a human head.[18] The ball was the individual property of the player and comprised part of his equipment (pp. 75, 77, 127, 151).

---

[17] Five translations of the Popol Vuh were consulted, namely those of Brasseur, of Jena, of Raynaud, of Villacorta and Rodas, and of Ximinez. Unless otherwise stated, page citations refer to Brasseur.

[18] The representations of players which have been consulted include figurines, large bas-reliefs from apron markers and panels, and the smaller reliefs on the face of alley markers. The list below, while admittedly not complete, is sufficiently representative for present purposes:

Figurines: Joyce, pl. V, figs .2, 3; pls. VII and VIII, figs. 1—5; Lothrop, 1923; Thompson, 1941, fig. 33b, f; 1943 a, fig. 1; Toscano, fig. 1. Ekholm, 1946, pls. 1, figs. c, d, 3, figs. a, b, f—h, and 4 covers many of the examples given by the first three authors and adds others as well.

Bas-reliefs: Satterthwaite, pl. IV, fig. 22, gives the principal earlier representation. Most of the other examples either fall without the cultural domain of the Maya or date from the Mexican period (Thompson, 1943 b) or later. Of the former, there is that at Tepatlaxco, Vera Cruz (Batres), of the latter, Santa Lucia Cozumalhuapa (Habel, Strebel) and Chichen Itzá (Great Court—Marquina,

Court *(hom):* The court of the Quiché legend comprises a flat play-ing area bordered by a taller structure bearing a recessed cornice or ledge (p. 169). That of the lords of Xibalba (the Underworld) is described as being adorned by a great pediment (Raynaud, p. 30). The textual evidence for the presence of houses about the court is ambiguous, al-though Lothrop has assumed that the molding or cornice presupposes such a construction.[19]

A great mass of information derived from excavations is now available as to the features of the Maya ball courts. While it is known that differences exist both in space and in time, it is not my purpose to enter into detailed discussion here. Some variations doubtless reflect archi-tectural styles, while others may have had a direct bearing upon the manner of play. It is with the latter that present concern chiefly lies; although even here only a brief summary of the principal characteristics of the Maya court will be attempted.

The courts thus far excavated lie within the ceremonial centers and generally share the orientation of the major structures therein. It is possible that a simpler form of court was also present in the satellite farming communities that are thought to have surrounded the centers. The Popol Vuh speaks of two youths playing in the court of their father (Raynaud, p. 51) or fathers (Brasseur, p. 131), but the inheritance suggested is that of tradition, rather than property. Such courts were in daily use (p. 131), and were swept clean prior to play.

The central feature of the Maya court is an alley bounded on either side by an elongated mound, or range, from the inner face of which a low bench projects to form the alley border. At either end, the alley opens into an expanded end-field, rectangular in shape and bounded by *termini* that range from a low wall or inner edge of a plaza to a stone line set flush with the surface. The plan of the court thus defined takes the form of a single, or more commonly a double T.[20] In profile, range and bench reveal similar variability. The bench may combine a vertical

p. 73 and associated plates; Monjas Court—Bolles, unpublished data; Red House—Ruppert, unpublished data).

Alley markers, on the other hand, frequently depict players; and many of them antedate the Mexican period. Mention may be made of those of Lubaantun (Thompson, 1941, note 7); Copan (Morley, 1937—8; also Ekholm, 1946, pl. 2); Cankuen (Morley, 1922, p. 123); and Chinkultic (Thompson, 1941, fig. 33, d; Ekholm, pl. 3, d). In most of the alley markers the size of the ball seems to have been exaggerated.

[19] Lothrop, 1927, p. 26. Villacorta and Rodas seem to have reached a similar conclusion. Such an interpretation is entirely in accord with the archeological facts; since buildings are frequently present on the ranges or at the ends of the court.

[20] The courts at Kaminaljuyú, in the Guatemala highlands, may have lacked the expanded end-zones, although Mr. A. Ledyard Smith has indicated in conversation (1947) that in some at least these features may have been present.

or sloping face with a horizontal or sloping top, surmounted in turn by a sloping apron and vertical wall, or simply by a vertical wall.[21]

While the gross dimensions of the courts, like other features, exhibit a wide range of variation, the great majority of them, setting aside considerations of time or place, fall within comparatively narrow limits.[22] This, in turn, argues a uniformity in such gross features of play as the number of participants in a game.

Of lesser features, mention may be made of the various markers with reference to which play seems to have been governed. These include paired markers set in the apron or on the face of the bench, in the form of panels at either end of the alley and opposite the center; markers, in the form of sculptured representations of animal or human heads, similarly located on the top of each range or the top of each bench; and unpaired markers located in the corresponding positions along the major axis of the alley. Excavated courts present combinations of these types of markers. In some late courts (e. g. Chichen Itzá) a stone line, set flush with the surface of the court, runs across the ends of the alleys. Undoubtedly, its function was analogous to that of the end members of paired or alley markers. In one early court (Cobá, in northern Yucatan), paired stone rings set into the top of each apron occur as center markers;

[21] Courts which combine a vertical wall with a sloping bench top (and more usually with a vertical, than a sloping, bench face) are widespread from southwestern Guatemala and adjacent Honduras and El Salvador northward through the central part of Yucatan to the major cities in the north of that peninsula. This corresponds to the type "B" of Acosta and Moedano Koer. Predominantly within the highlands of Chiapas and Guatemala, but present on the fringes of the first type in Yucatan and British Honduras, are courts which present an apron and vertical wall in combination with a sloping bench top (and usually an inclined bench face). According to the above classification, this is type "A". In only a few sites, and those chiefly of the Mexican period, does a vertical wall combine with a horizontal bench top (type "C").

Nomenclature for court features follows principally Satterthwaite, pt. IV, with additions from Acosta and Moedano Koer.

[22] To mention but two important dimensions for which information is available, a mean alley length of from 16 to 35 meters (52.5—115 feet) is generally combined with a corresponding breadth of from ca. 6 to 9 meters (19.7—29.5 feet). The data, expressed in meters, are as follows:

Length of Alley	Average Breadth of Alley	No. of Courts
below 5	0.6	5
6—10	3.5	3
11—15	6.0	3
16—20	5.8	17
21—25	6.8	16
26—30	8.5	12
31—35	8.8	7
36—40	11.0	5
41—80	9.3	4
above 80	35.0	1

while all other courts that exhibit this feature clearly reflect Mexican influence. Raynaud (p. 30, note 2) has seen in the *baté*, which in the Popol Vuh forms an invariable component of the player's equipment, a ring which he equates with the paired rings of these courts. Under the assumption that such rings were necessary for play (in the Mexican game, they serve as goals), Raynaud sees in the *baté* a portable form which was set into the wall prior to play. The idea is further expanded by Blom.[23] The data which have led several authorities to reject this interpretation, (with which rejection I find myself in agreement) will be discussed in detail in further sections.[24]

Common to many Maya courts is the presence of associated buildings on one or both of the ranges, fronting the court. They sometimes occur at either end of the court, but combinations of lateral and terminal temples are not unknown. Whatever the position, their function is probably to house images of associated deities and ceremonial paraphernalia and to act as a place within which to perform the attendant rites. Some may also have functioned as a stand from which dignitaries could observe the game. Neither textual nor archeological testimony, however, serves to define the function of these structures.

Players: There is no mention of women as players, nor do they appear in the sculptural representations. Uniformly, the participants are men. Bishop Landa specifies (p. 124) that the game was a favorite with young, unmarried men, who came together to play; and this picture finds agreement in the Popol Vuh (p. 71). On the other hand, it need not be assumed that all players were drawn from this group. Each player owned the equipment he used, which comprised ball *(quiq)*, ring *(baté)*, hip-

---

[23] Blom, 1932, p. 513f. Not all of the translators of the Popol Vuh have rendered *baté* as "ring." Villacorta and Rodas equate it with "lance", while Ximinez leaves it in the native form. Both Schuller and Thompson, as will be shown below, consider the *baté* a part of the players garb.

Blom calls attention to the Tainan word, *batey*, in its sense of "court," as a suggestive parallel to the Quiché homonym. Should the two words prove to be historically related, the interpretation of *baté* as a court feature, i.e. the side-ring, would be logical. But, as Las Casas makes clear, the Antillean term is applied to the ball and to the game, as well as to the court. The Arawaken cognates suggested for the term would make reference to the ball basic, with the others derivative. The chance of a genetic connection with the Quiché word accordingly becomes more remote.

[24] While no detailed analysis of the distribution of secondary ball-court features will be attempted here, discussion of the occurrence of some characteristics should prove of value. Alley markers to my knowledge are unreported from the southern highlands of Guatemala and Chiapas. Paired markers in the form of heads seem at present to be southerly, ranging from the Guatemala highlands and Honduras into British Honduras. Paired rings, on the other hand, are restricted to late sites in Yucatan, with the exception of Cobá, already mentioned (Thompson et al.) and Naco, a late Nahuatl site in Honduras (see Strong et al.).

leather *(tzuun)*, glove *(pachgab)*, and headgear *(yachvach)*, the latter provided with casque or face net *(vachzot)*.[25] Representations of ball players (see fn. 18 above) show a heavy girdle, or broad belt, which is woven of such a width as to approximate a corselet, though it is more usually narrow. It ranges in position from the waist to a place just beneath the armpits, being secured by a tie on one side or behind the player. Beneath it, the kilt-like hip leather covers the thighs, but is cut away in front for freedom of movement. Gloves are shown on one hand or on both. At times they cover the hand, but more usually they take the form of a wrapping or of a quilted guard for the lower arm. When the player is shown in action, the glove is worn on the arm corresponding to the hip with which the ball is struck. Headdresses appear frequently; but only the Lubaantun figurines depict what can be distinguished as a casque. The head net fails to win a place among the representations, although this may possibly arise from an artistic reluctance to conceal the player's face. To some degree the elaborate headdresses so often shown may be ceremonial garb, to be discarded in the actual game. They do not appear on the Piedras Negras reliefs.[26]

An item upon which the Popol Vuh is silent, but for which almost every figurine or bas relief gives testimony, is the knee pad. Occasionally a player is shown with a pad on each knee. In the majority of cases, however, only one is worn, usually, though here again there are exceptions, on the right knee. There seems to be a correspondence in the wearing of belt, knee pad, and glove, apparently dependent upon the manner of play. The player wears the glove and the knee pad on the side with which he strikes the ball, and ties the ring either on the

[25] Joyce has interpreted as ball players certain figurines from Lubaantun which wear a glove on the right hand, hip leather, perhaps to be equated with the *tzuun*, together with a helmet-like device that leaves only eyes and nose visible. They appear on Pls. VII and VIII, figs. 1—5, of his work. Similar figurines, from San Pedro and San Antonio, Toledo, British Honduras, were on display in 1947 at the Chicago Natural History Museum.

Two other figurines, also shown by Joyce — who, however, terms them warriors — more closely approximate other Maya representations of the ball player, particularly as to the girdle. These examples (pl. V, figs. 2,5) lack gloves; and their fragmentary character unfortunately does not permit a statement as to the headgear. Ekholm (1946, pl. 3, g, h) also considers them to represent ball players.

Schuller (p. 110) is authority for considering the *vachzot* to be, not a casque, but a face net. In his opinion, the ring, *baté*, is a neckring, since it contains the element, *-te*, neck; and he postulates that it was used to secure the lower edge of the net. Thompson (1941, p. 324), while offering evidence that tends to corroborate this view, himself believes that the *baté* is the leather girdle or belt worn over the hip leather.

Evidence that has led me to agree with Thompson's interpretation is presented in the section devoted to the manner of playing.

[26] Satterthwaite, 1933—4, pt. IV, fig. 22.

other side or behind him. Artistic license and the dictates of symmetry no doubt account for the relatively high proportion of left-handedness thus depicted.

Regional variation might be summoned up to explain the absence of the knee pad in the Quiché account, but it seems more likely that it was thought too insignificant for mention.

When it was not in use, the player hung his equipment from the rafters of his dwelling (p. 79).

Teams: While the Popol Vuh contains a sequence in which one hero competes against two opponents (pp. 71, 151, 153), the sides are more usually equal, with one or two players on a team. The reliefs at the Mexican period courts of Chichen Itzá, on the other hand, depict ceremonial processions in which a greater number of individuals, clad as players, appear. This suggests that more sizeable teams might have existed.

Wagers: An obscure passage describes a pre-game dispute over both the wager and the ball to be used (p. 151). Raynaud (p. 54, note 3) has indicated that each side had undoubtedly prepared its ball magically; and this may well have been a factor in the desire of each side that its own ball be used. An additional reason for anxiety is suggested by evidence that the owners of the ball has first service (Brasseur, p. 153, Raynaud, p. 59).

Play: First service fell to the side that provided the ball, coincident, in this case, with the home team (Brasseur, p. 151, Raynaud, p. 59). The visitors won a point, whereupon it was agreed to use their ball, and thus give them the serve for the next play (?) (pp. 151—3). Service would appear to have gone to the side that had just scored.

The manner in which the ball was struck is somewhat difficult to resolve, chiefly because of differing interpretations which have been placed upon the *baté*. This object figures largely in the play: the ball is described as striking it, passing through it, and so forth, according to the interpretation placed upon the Quiché word by the translator. As I have already mentioned, Schuller (p. 110) thinks of it as a neck ring; and this, taken together with the helmeted figures from Lubaantun, might well lead one to ask, was the ball struck with the head among the Maya? In the light of the data already adduced for regions to the south and east, where this method of play predominates, an affirmative conclusion would be significant.

Unfortunately for this identification, the sculptural evidence runs counter to it. The ball player in action is characteristically represented as resting upon his padded knee, or in midair, meeting the ball with one hip, legs bent beneath him to take the fall on the corresponding knee, while with gloved arm bent upward he protects his face or, less likely, prepares for a follow-through. If the Popol Vuh uniformly describes the ball as striking the "ring," the reliefs with equal consistency show it striking the broad belt about the waist of the player. It seems difficult to avoid the conclusion that they are one and the same.

Aside from what has already been mentioned, there is little evidence for use of the hand or arm, and none for use of the shoulder, in returning the ball.

Scoring: Discussion of the method by which the Maya scored has usually centered about the ring, baté, which, as has been pointed out, Raynaud and Blom identify with the paired rings, set into the side walls of some courts, through which the ball must be put. The argument here is through analogy with the accounts of early chroniclers, describing the cognate game of the Mexicans. Thompson has shown convincingly that the pertinent passages of the Popol Vuh (pp. 151–3, 169) cannot logically be construed in this manner.[27] Moreover, an alternative solution to the method of scoring does appear in the former of these passages. In that instance, the players of Xibalba serve the ball, which strikes the ring (i. e. belt) of one of the heroes and goes bounding about on the floor of the court: wherefore the heroes lose. It seems to me permissable to deduce that the scoring was here based upon the fact that the ball went dead on the losers' side of the court.[28]

Although, to judge from the same description, a single score might be construed as ending the game, play was resumed and was not brought to an end until the victors had won two goals out of three played (p. 153). The number of points appears to have been arrived at by joint agreement by both parties.

Ceremonial associations: While the game undoubtedly possessed its secular side, being counted as a popular sport (p. 71), there is good evidence that it also had strong religious and ceremonial connotations. The mythology of the Popol Vuh carries it to the Lords of the Underworld (Xibalba), who had their own court. Although this plainly reflects an extension of mundane values and pursuits to the sphere of the gods, it is significant that it was the ball game that was selected. With regard to other associated deities information is regrettably scant. Joyce states (probably by analogy with the Mexican data) that Quetzalcoatl in particular was linked up with the game; and he sees an evolution of the long nose of Eecatl, in whose guise that deity often appears, out of the helmet worn by the ball-player figurines of Lubaantun.[29]

The archeological remains likewise testify to the ceremonial character of the Maya ball game. The inclusion of ball courts within ceremonial

[27] Thompson, 1941, p. 324.
[28] In the second description of play (p. 169), the hero, Xbalanque, returns the serve, sending the ball above the court to lodge in a cornice. There is no mention of the scoring of this stroke.
[29] Joyce, 1933, p. xxii.

centers, the association of special temples with the courts, and the symbolism of decorative features, together with the elaborate headdresses which adorn most of the ball players represented in figurines and reliefs, all lead to the same conclusion. Ekholm has recently revived the hypothesis which would identify the stone yokes of eastern Mexico and the southern highlands with the ball game belts depicted archeologically.[30] If the interpretation which he has so cogently urged be accepted, and it should be remembered that alternative explanations exist, the stone yokes would doubtless be added to the stock of formal elements worn in rituals associated with the ball court.

Still another feature, but one which blends physiological and ritual elements, may turn out to be casually associated with the ball game. At two sites thus far, structures identified as sweat houses have been reported that occur in proximity to ball courts.[31] The possibility accordingly exists that players may have sought to purify body and soul in the sweat house as part of a pre-game ritual.

Indeed, it would be strange to find among the Maya an institution as prominent as the ball game that had not become suffused with the prevailing ceremonialism. Yet, withal it retained secular functions that are clearly perceptible. The Popol Vuh depicts it as a sport played by

[30] Ekholm, 1946. Since this was written, Ekholm has suggested (1949) that palmate stones, found principally in the Totonac area, and thin stone heads which range from Tampico south to El Salvador and Honduras, may have been worn in the broad protective belt of the ball player, in ceremonies associated with the ball court. He points (p. 8 f.) to a possible cognate for the former in the rods thrust in the ventral portion of the belt of the figures in the friezes of the Great Court at Chichen Itzá (Palacios, 1937, fig. 41). Attention may be called to an even closer analogy in a clay figurine illustrated by Morley (1946, pl. 82, lower left) as coming from the island of Jaina, northwestern coast of Yucatan, and dating from the end of the Old Empire (Thompson's Initial Series period). It may be that this figurine records influences from regions farther to the north. The player is represented as wearing ear disks and necklace, a broad belt fastened with a narrow strip tied around it, hip leathers and a pad on the right knee. Arms are broken, hence the presence of gloves cannot be ascertained. A spatulate object with a knob at the top, similar in general outline to the palmate stones, is thrust through the belt so that its lower tip covers the genetalia — which it may perhaps be designed to protect. Although the mode of wearing does not conform with that postulated for palmate stones by Ekholm, it does accord with that shown by the small figure in his Fig. 1, a.

[31] Piedras Negras: Court R-11 and Structure R-13 (immediately adjacent): Court K-6 and Structure N-1 (opposite end of plaza): Satterthwaite, 1933—4, Pt. 1, map.

Chichen Itzá: Court 3 E 2 and sweat bath No. 2; but cf. sweat bath No. 1, not so associated: Ruppert, unpubl. notes and Morley, 1946, pl. 39.

While it is evident that these data do not indicate an exclusive association of sweat house and ball court, they do suggest an occasional tendency in that direction. The paucity of information on this subject may merely reflect the limited number of sweat houses identified as such to date. See Cresson, 1938.

tribesmen and as an inter-community activity. In the latter role, the game forms the chief part of a group of ordeals that the visitor must undergo in order to prove himself in the eyes of his hosts. Manifestly, we are dealing in this instance with an episode that is highly charged with mythological content; nonetheless it serves well to emphasize the competitive nature of the Maya game. In the hands of the lords of the Underworld that game becomes a fit instrument for aggression. So clearly is this apparent to the victorious heroes that they forbid the conquered lords to play from that time on (p. 189). It is perhaps in a kindred light that one must view the friezes associated with the Great Ball Court at Chichen Itzá, with their scenes of struggle between Toltec and Maya and with the eventual submission of the latter.[32] Truth to tell, these and similar panels at Chichen Itzá in themselves must reflect an alien influence; yet they are not so foreign to the Maya concept of the game, as reflected in the Quiché legend, as one might at first suppose.

Lexical addenda: The presence in the manuscript Tzeldal dictionary of de Guzman (1620) of terms relating to the ball game, and to other games as well, has led me to compile a list of similar terms in cognate dialects and languages. While no attempt has been made to exhaust all possibilities, the resultant list provides a representative sample. In each case the original orthography has been retained.

Tzeldal (de Guzman):

Juego de pelotacō las nalgas, game of ball with the hips: *sū olim pitz.*[33]
Jugar ala pelota ut olin, to play ball (as with the rubber ball?): *xpitzibō.* cf. Juego de fortuna como jugabā olim cō frisoles o cañas, game of fortune (played) as they used to play ball etc.
Jugador asi, one who plays thus: *pitzibil*
Peloto como quiera, any ball: *pitz*
Pelota quellos usaban, the ball they used: *chich*

[32] Tozzer, 1928, p. 164. Several of the courts at Chichen Itzá depict, along the face of the bench, processions which meet at the center line. In the best preserved of these, that at the Great Court (Palacios, fig. 41 and p. 73) there are seven members on each side, armed and clad in ceremonial garb that includes such items of the ball player's gear as arm ruffs, knee pad on the right knee, and in some cases what may be the broad belt. The two files, which are distinctive in certain items of dress, meet at a disk bearing upon its surface a skull. Across this symbol, the leader of one group has decapitated his foe kneeling opposite with a knife and, while the blood gushes from the trunk, holds the severed head of his victim. Similar scenes may be represented at other courts at the same site (Red House, Ruppert, unpublished notes; Monjas, Bolles, unpublished notes). Strongly analogous are the friezes on the bench of the court at Tajín, in the Totonac area (Spinden, 1933), while legend and practice within the Valley of Mexico likewise contains the element of human sacrifice. It is striking that the sequence in the Great Court shows both sides armed: here evidently is no mere record of offering, but the sacrifice of a conquered foe.

[33] *"Olim"* appears to be related neither to gum (goma — *xuch*) nor to hip (nalga — *ytil. quit. abit*: L. honestius *nactghabal. gnactaghib.*)

Sangre, blood: *chihch, qchihchel*
Juego de pelota conlas manos, game of ball with the hands: *paxpax*
Jugar ala pelota conlas manos, to play ball with the hands: *qpoxbu*
Jugador asi, one who plays thus: *ghpoxbighel*
Jugo [sic] de pelota [illegible] con los pies, game of ball with the feet: *poliz*
Jugar ala pelota dandole conlos pies, to play ball striking it with the feet: *xpoçibō*
Jugador asi, one who plays thus: *poçibil, poçinom*[34]

Maya (Pio Perez):

El juego de la pelota, the ball game, the ball court: *pok yak*
Jugar pelota, saltar y el salto, to play ball, to leap and the leap; *pok*
Jugar a la pelota, to play ball: *pitz*
Pelota, ball: *pok*
Arrojarlo ó abarrajarlo contra la pared, to hurl it or send it against the wall: *pokchintah*
Pelotear la pelota, to play ball: *pokolpoktah*[35]
...Toda cosa redonde, anything round: *uol, uolob*[36]
Sangre, sangre cuajada, blood, coagulated blood: *olom*
Sangre cuajada, coagulated blood: *olomkik*: sangre, blood: *kik, kiik*
El árbol que produce la goma elástica y otro especie de árbol, the tree that yields elastic gum, and other kinds of trees: *kiikché*
For comparison with Quiché *hom*, court, cf. hoyo que deja el hundimiento de una cosa hueca, cavity left by the collapse of a hollow object; *hom, homil*; and cosa ancha, broad thing: *homocuac.*
The Maya dictionary of Beltram gives the following: Juego de pelota, ball game (court): *pok yah, okelek*; and pelota, ball: *pok.* Quiché terms are to be found in the text of the preceding sections.
Mam (Reynoso) offers for comparison only: Goma de arbol, resin of a tree: *vuiix.*
Motul (Martinez) gives: Sangre, blood: *kik, olom.*
Huastec (Tapia Zenteno) gives: Pelota, ball: *mule.*

In summary of the lexical data it may be said that the Tzeldal material offers strong evidence for the existence of three ball games clearly distinguishable on the basis of the manner in which the ball is struck. That employing the hips, and thus inferentially to be identified with the game depicted in reliefs, is designated by employment of the morpheme *pitz*, which is likewise generally the term for ball; and the morpheme *olim* also appears to be restricted to the same game. For the

---

[34] The three types of game appear to be lexically distinct, embodying respectively the roots *pitz *pox, and *poc. In addition, the rubber-ball game is characterized by the morpheme, "*olim.*"

[35] While the majority of the structures examined contain the morpheme, *pok, the appearance of the element, *pitz, suggests an analogy with Tzeldal, where the morphemes, *pox and *pitz present parallels. In Tzeldal, as has been shown, these roots refer respectively to a game played with the hand and one played by striking with the hip. Did a similar distinction exist among the Maya-speaking peoples of Yucatan? The evidence to date is insufficient to establish this point.

[36] cf. Voluntad, albredio..., will: *uolah, olah.*

game employing the hands, *pox is the characteristic element. That in which the feet propel the ball appears to be set apart by the element, *poç. The appearance of distinct native roots intimate that the three games were probably aboriginal in origin. The Tzeldal name for the ball, *chich*, doubtless designates a rubber ball, since the term appears to arise from an analogy between blood and the oozings of the rubber tree. It is uncertain, however, whether the same ball was used in all three games.

Parallels in the Maya dialect (notably the appearance of *pitz and *pok as synonyms) suggest that a similar situation may have existed elsewhere. Other dialects merely serve to confirm the linkage existing between *chich* and the rubber tree and to point to *olim* as an occasional synonym.

CHAPTER FOUR

THE GAMES IN MEXICO
AND THE SOUTHWESTERN UNITED STATES

Peoples of Southern and Central Mexico

To the north of the Maya, the ball game was played by diverse peoples of southern Mexico, in Oaxaca and Guerrero, and of the Southeast Central Mesa and in Michoacan; along the eastern littoral in Vera Cruz, ranging perhaps as far north as Tamaulipas; and, on the west coast, in South Sinaloa to the Fuerte-Yaqui Lowland, as well as the corresponding regions of the Sierra del Nayarit and Central Sierra Madre.[1] The western extension reappears, after a lacuna, in northern Sonora and the southwestern United States as far as northern Arizona. The evidence upon which the Mexican distribution rests is in part eye-witness reports, in part archeological findings. For the Southwest, it is entirely archeological. Since ethnological material for southern and central Mexico is not always capable of being separated, I propose to treat them together here, while indicating such differences as are distinguishable. The west coast manifestations will be treated in a subsequent section, as will also the extension into the southwestern United States.

The contemporaneous evidence for central and southern Mexico takes two forms. There is, first of all, a large body of accounts written by Europeans and by natives after the Conquest. While presumably many of them apply specifically to the game in the Valley of Mexico (Southeast Central Mesa), a number of others are not so assignable and may refer equally to the areas to the south. The second type of evidence is pictorial, in the form of codices which depict the game in progress. In the description to follow, the native terms given are those of the Aztecs (Nahuatl).

Although a number of writers have left us accounts of the ball game, their descriptions are not of equal value, and many have patently drawn their data, and sometimes even the text in full, from their predecessors. It seems clear that the following lines of literary indebtedness exist:

1. Motolinia (Toribio de Benavente), dated after 1541, was copied directly by Zorita (ca. 1584). A sketch of Motolinia's activities has already been given see ch. 3, fn. 16 above.

2. Gómara, must have obtained his own information from one of the followers of Cortez, since he himself was never in the New World. Since his account in

[1] Divisions follow Kroeber, 1939, especially Map 6.

some details coincides with that of Motolinia, it is possible that he had the opportunity to see the latter's description before he himself published (1552). He is followed by Cervantes Salazar (1561), Herrera (1601—15), Torquemada (after 1613), Solis (1684), and Clavigero (1780). Of the subsidiary accounts, those of Torquemada and Cervantes Salazar are of greatest value, since the writers were in a position to check at first hand the accuracy of their description.

3. Sahagun was in Mexico by 1529 and had opportunity to witness the game at first hand prior to its abolition. His account, however, is surprisingly meager for so careful an investigator and it adds little to what other sources tell us.

4. Durán, published in 1585, combines direct observation with detailed reporting to produce an exceedingly valuable account of the Mexican game. As we have already seen, Joyce is of the opinion that his description may also apply to the Late Maya. Certain details of description do, indeed, suggest observations in southern Mexico.

5. Alvarado Tezozomoc (fl. 1598), scion of native Aztec royalty, presents a significantly variant account, in which he is followed by Veytia (fl. 1778).

6. For the neighboring kingdom of Tlaxcala, Camargo, a noble Tlaxcalatec mestizo, writing in the early years after the Conquest, likewise gives an independent description which will be considered separately. In this, he does not vary substantially from the information given by the Spaniards.

7. Peter Martyr, who as a member of the Council of the Indies had available to him all the records of the colonies, presents in his *Decades* (1530) an account of the ball game in Mexico which, it must be admitted, is at some variance with the statements of eye witnesses.

Since the early chroniclers described what they saw in terms of the games then popular in Europe, a brief characterization of the latter may not be amiss. Four ball games then current in Spain are distinguished by Covarrubias Orozco in his *Tesoro de la lengua castellana* published in 1673:

PELOTA, instrumento conocido con que se juega. Ay muchas diferencias de pelotas; pero la ordinaria es, la que està embutida con pelos, de donde tomô el nombre. Tiene figura redôda, y està hecha de quartos. Con esta se juega en los trinquetes, y por esta razon se llamô trigonal, pelota chica de sobrecuerda. Esta era la pelota cortesana que se jugaua con la palma a mano abierta. Era a proposito para los moços, por la presteza, y ligereza que quiere. Otra era de viento, que llamaron follis, esta se jugaua en lugares espaciosos, assi en calle, como en corredores largos. La tercera se llamô paganica, porque la usauan los villanes en sus aldeas. Era embutida de pluma. A la quarta dixeron harpasso, ô harpasto. Esta se jugaua casi como aora la chueca, porque se ponian tantos a tantos, diuidiendo el campo, y hazian sus pinas, y el que por entre las dos del contrario passaua êl harpasto ganaua, y el que la arrebataua iba corriendo con ella, el contrario acudia a detenerle hasta venir a la lucha.

We may omit *harpasto*, a game roughly equivalent to hockey, from further consideration, since our sources are in agreement in denying resemblances between it and the Mexican game. Of the others, *paganica*, the rural game, not improbably represents a local manifestation of the basic game involving the use of a stuffed ball, from which the divergent games of tennis (the *jeu de paume* of France) and *pelota vasca* (the modern Basque game of *jai alai*) evolved. Consequently, we shall center description on tennis, of which we have fairly old rule books, devoting only a few remarks to *pelota vasca*.

Tennis, the game of courtiers, had spread from France into neighboring kingdoms several centuries prior to the discovery of the New World, bringing with it a court *(trinquete)* embodying special features. Covarrubias thus describes it.

> *TRINQVETE*, el juego de pelota cubierto, quales son los de los corredores; dixose assi, quasi trinquete, por los tres angulos que tiene cerrados, dos en el dentro, y uno en el fuera.

In plan, the court was rectangular, an average value being about 100 feet by 30 feet; and the floor was enclosed by two end walls and lateral walls designated as main and side walls. A penthouse ran along both end and side walls, projecting out upon the floor, and bearing a series of galleries and doors in its side-wall course. Across the middle of the court there was hung a transverse net, dividing it into service and hazard sides. Within the end penthouse of the service side was a long opening known as the *dedans*, while in the right-hand corner (as seen from the service court) of the corresponding hazard penthouse was the *grille*; and these, together with the end galleries of the side penthouse constituted the winning holes. Just in front of the *grille* there projected from the main, or right-hand, wall a buttress known as the *tambour*. Other features, present in the French court, were less frequently accepted abroad. Of the lines drawn in the court, we need only mention the chief ones, a play line to delimit the upper boundary of the walls, the hazard and service lines, which enclosed the service area of the court, and the chase lines, drawn at equal intervals parallel to the end walls.

Play, as Crawley has pointed out,[2] was much affected by the need to make the hard, leather-covered ball rebound. In service, it was driven with the palm of the hand or a racquet against the side penthouse, to drop into the hazard court. A good return involved recovering the ball before the second bound, and sending it over the net, to land within the opponent's court or to strike his walls within the play line. A player lost a stroke if he hit the ball twice in succession or permitted the ball to touch his person. He scored a point by sending the ball into one of the winning openings on the other side, by receiving two consecutive faulty serves, when his opponent failed to return the ball, and when he won a chase.

To set up a chase, the player let the ball pass him, whereupon the presiding marker would call out the chase line nearest which the ball struck on its second bounce. The closer to the back wall, the better was the chase. A stroke into the rival's galleries or doors (save the winning gallery) also counted as a chase. A chase did not establish a score, but had to be played off; and thus several accumulated chases might be

[2] Crawley, 1914, p. xviii.

resolved in sequence. The chase was won by driving the ball into a. winning opening or by making a better chase, i. e. one closer to the end wall, than had the opponent.

A match comprised the best of three or five sets, each in turn made up of six or eight games. The vantage, or final, set must be won by a margin of two games. A game consisted of four winning strokes, scored 15, 30, 40, and game. A score tied at 40 was termed deuce and must be won by two strokes in succession, otherwise the player dropped back to deuce.

Teams usually were made up of only one or two individuals, so that the grace and skill of the player were as sharply exhibited as in any courtly demonstration of athletic prowess. Correspondingly, handicaps stressed restrictions of play rather than compensatory spotting of scores. Wagers were customary and might become extravagant. Popular alike with laity and with the worldly clergy of the court, tennis presents a prevailing secular, essentially sportive, aspect in Europe of the sixteenth to eighteenth centuries.[3]

Pelota vasca, of which there are a number of variants, depending upon the form of the court and the implement (hand, glove, paddle, or *chistera*) with which the ball is struck. The court is now known as *frontón*, a name formerly applied in Spain to the end wall.[4] Basically, there are two walls, an end wall *(frontis)* and a side wall *(ble)*. A back wall *(rebote)* may also be added, as well as a fourth wall, but these are optional. Upon the *ble*, vertical lines are drawn at intervals *(cuadros)* of four meters, starting from the *frontis*. There may be between fifteen and twenty such *cuadros*, which correspond to the chase lines of tennis. Transversely across the floor *(cancha)* two lines run from the fourth and seventh *cuadros*. These serve the same general purpose as do the service and hazard lines in the tennis court. *Escases*, equivalent to the play line, run along the walls and upon the open sides of the court.

The object of the game is much as in tennis, although the special characteristics of the court involve some differences in play. In general, play is by rebound against the walls, in particular the *frontis*, and the ball must be taken on the first bound. Faults include, among others, body fouls and bouncing the ball out of the court. The 19th century development of the *chistera*, a long, curved basket, worn on the hand, has led to changes in play. Officials include an umpire, a scorekeeper, and perhaps other.[5]

Finally, mention must be made of the games played with the *follis*,

[3] See: Heathcote, 1890; Whitman, 1932; Encyclopedia Brittanica, 14th ed.: Lawn Tennis and Tennis; and Divertissemens innocens, 1696, pp. 333—59, for a contemporary French description.

[4] See: Gattel, 1790; Fronton: Real Academia Española, 1803. Both appear to apply the term to the end wall of a tennis court.

[5] Espasa: 1914—35, *Pelota*.

a leather ball containing an inflated bladder. To some extent, the *pelota de viento*, as it was known in Spain, seems to have entered into handball, and perhaps tennis, at least on the Iberian Peninsula. The chief game was that known in Italy as *pallone*, a game which has been traced back to Roman prototypes. By the 13th century it had entered France, and it is claimed that it was also in Spain by the 15th century. With respect to this last point, however there is some doubt, for Oviedo describes it as an exotic game. "In Italy, when I was there," he observes, "I saw them play a game with a very large ball, as large as a jar of arroba capacity [a variable measure equivalent to 25 pounds in weight] or larger, and they call it *balon* or *palon*. And in particular I saw it many times in Lombardy and in Naples among well-bred men; and they struck that ball or *balon* with the foot...."[6]

There were several variant forms of this game. It might be played in an open field,[7] in a courtyard or room,[8] or, as described by Covarrubias, it might involve the use of a street or broad corridor. A transverse line divided the court into two halves and chase lines were drawn. Play in an enclosed space involved rebound from the side wall.[9] The ball, of which modern examples have a diameter of about five inches (cf. Oviedo's remarks), might be struck with a wooden club *(scanno)* or a spiked gauntlet *(bracciale)*, or it might be kicked. Drives of up to one hundred yards are reported to have been made.[10] In comparison to tennis, it was a far slower game.

These games, then, constituted the cultural referents in terms of which t̠ ͻ early observers sought to describe the similar games of the New V͘orld. The courtly associations of tennis, as well as its outright popularity, make it probable that many comparisons were drawn with it, particularly by those who in Spain had frequented the royal capital. Hidalgos, on the other hand, might be more apt to speak in terms of *pelota*, which fortunately shares many similarities with tennis, or of *pallone*.

The Mexican game they described may be summarized as follows:[11]

Game: The name generally assigned to the game is *ulamaliztli* (M, G), likened by Motolinia to the Spanish game of the inflated ball.

Ball, *olin, olli, ulli, ule*, etc., whence Spanish *hule*: The ball received its name from its substance, the gum of a tree that grew in the tierra

[6] Oviedo, vol. 1, bk. 5, ch. 2, p. 166 (translation mine).
[7] See Crawley, 1914.   [8] Heathcote, 1890, fig. 1.
[9] Crawley, 1914, p. xviii.   [10] Heathcote, 1890, p. 10.
[11] See: Motolinia (M), 1903, pt. 4, ch. 25, pp. 337—9; Zorita, ch. 26, pp. 307—10; Gomara (G), ch. 93, pp. 215—7; Cervantes Salazar (CS), bk. 4, ch. 6, pp. 13—4; Herrera, bk. 7, ch. 8, pp. 181—2; Torquemada (T), vol. 2, bk. 14, ch. 12, pp. 552—4; Solis, vol. 1, bk. 3, ch. 15, p. 278; Clavigero, vol. 2, pp. 213—5; Sahagun (S), bk. 3, ch. 10, pp. 297—9; bk. 8, ch. 17, p. 320; Durán (D), vol. 2, ch. 101, pp. 242—6; Tezozomoc (Tez), ch. 2, pp. 227—9; Veytia, vol. 1, bk. 2, ch. 13, pp. 296—8; Camargo (C), ch. 16, p. 135f.; Martyr (Ma), Dec. 5, bk. 10, ch. 5, p. 469.

caliente (M, G, D).[12] The tree was tapped and the exuding white resin collected (M, G). Coagulation was induced, or hastened, by cooking the latex with herbs (D), the end product being black in color (M, G).[13] The ball seems to have been shaped by hand, as in the Antilles (M) although we have no details.[14] The finished object was almost certainly solid (G) and of the size of a small bowling ball (D). While heavier than a hollow ball (M, G), it possessed superior qualities of resiliency that were constantly singled out for comment.[15]

Court *(tlachtli, tlachco, tlacho, ollamaloyan)*: The principal ball court of each town was located in the market place, with lesser ones in the *barrios* (M). Gómara tells us that the owner was always a noble, Cervantes Salazar that he was a noble or chief, remarks that one would do well to view against the then feudal structure of Spain. Duran seems to imply that the courts were built as a civic enterprise, which suggests that the proprietorship exercised by these leaders arose principally from their civic status.[16] Other courts were located in temple compounds:

[12] The list of tribute paid annually to the Tenochcan ruler, as depicted in the Codex Mendoza (fol. 45 v., 46 r.) includes 16,000 rubber balls sent by twenty-two towns in southern Mexico. As Blom (p. 398) has pointed out, these tributaries lay on the eastern slopes of the Oaxacan mountains and in the adjacent Gulf lowlands, the region traditionally assigned to the Olmecs.

[13] Martyr states that "Las pelotas son de jugo de cierta hierba que trepa por pos árboles como el lúpulo por los setos..." (p. 469). The remainder of his description is, however, in accord with the statements of other writers.

[14] Las Casas, 1909, p. 159.

[15] Sahagun's reference to the game as "pelota de viento" may be ascribed to an implied analogy with the European game, rather than a description of the ball itself. From the time of Gómara on, writers expressed it as their belief that the distinctive method of striking the ball with the hips arose from the weight and hardness of the ball, which made use of the hands impracticable. While such reasoning appears inadequate, it does emphasize the factors that may have made for relative uniformity in the dimensions of the ball.

A gauge of the average size is suggested by Gómara's statement that the hole in the stone ring through which the ball could barely pass, was as large as an orange. Better figures may be derived from the values for a series of such rings (Blom, 1932, p. 498, note 15) for the hole of which measurements range from 16 to 31 cm. (6.3 to 12.2 inches). One example has an aperture of only 8 cm. (3.2 inches). In most of the codices the ball is represented as being somewhat smaller than a man's head.

Veytia (fl. 1778) states that in his time the ball was made lighter and of truer form by building it up about a core of wool. Since Clavigero, writing at about the same time, remarks that the old Mexican game was no longer played in central Mexico, it is questionable whether the new type of ball was used in that game. Veytia adds that in the old days the ball was of solid rubber and ranged upward in size from a diameter of about a span (8").

[16] This is not, of course, to deny the honored position of the ball game among the nobility, a position analogus to that occupied by tennis in the capitals of Europe. The point is that such associations in Mexico were neither invariable nor exclusively true.

thus Sahagun describes the *teotlachco* and *tezcatlachco*, the two courts within the temple compound of Huitzilopochtli and Tlaloc.[17] The archeological evidence, both for southern and eastern, as well as for central Mexico, is in accord with these statements and emphasizes the difficulty attendant upon efforts to draw a line defining exclusively secular from purely religious functions in these community centers.

Descriptions of the courts take two forms: in one (G), it is termed a low hall that is low and broad (i. e. the end zones ?), narrow and high (the alley and ranges ?); in the other (M), it is likened to a street (i. e. the alley – *tlamantli*) running between two thick walls (the side walls – *tlachmatl*, sing). Both sources agree in stating that the side walls diverged as they rose, so that the court was broader at the top than at the base. This may allude to the bench which extended into the court along either side wall. The end walls were lower (M, G). Stairs led up to the top of the walls (M). In plan the court comprised a narrow alley between the side walls, widening out beyond them into broad end zones (D). The resultant capital "I", or opposed capital "T," form is invariably presented in the native codices. Both walls and floor were kept clean and well plastered (M, G, D).[18] Values for the dimensions of the court range from a breadth of 20 to 30 feet and a length of 40 to 50 feet, measured only between the side walls (S),[19] to a breadth of between 100 and 150 feet and a length

[17] Bk. 2, appendix, pp. 223, 224. In the Codex Florentino, Sahagun's informant has simplified the picture somewhat, showing (Estampa XI) only one of the courts.

Chavero (vol. 1, p. 791) asserts that the two courts in question were dedicated respectively to the sun and moon.

[18] It is not amiss to point out that distinctions are clearly drawn by several of the chroniclers between the side walls and others which are most probably the end walls. Motolinia says, "las paredes de los lados eran bien altas y anchas: de las fronteras eran bajitas..." (p. 337). Gomara, followed by such men as Cervantes Salazar and Torquemada, says that the court was "mas alta á los lados que a las fronteras..." (p. 216).

"Frontera," in the sense of "facing," is used by Motolinia of the images of the gods, which he said were placed "encima de las paredes del *tlachco*, en el medio, el uno frontero del otro..." (p. 337); and it is similarly used by Durán when speaking of the two rings "fijadas en la pared frontera la una de la otra..." (p. 243).

In this sense it might have been applied to the benches, which could validly be considered two lower walls "facing" each other. On the other hand, in its connotation of "boundary", or "terminal," it could better be construed by end walls, which, as we already know from the archeological evidence, were indeed lower. The English translator of Gómara, writing (1578) less than thirty years after Gómara's first edition (1552), rendered that courtier's tennis terms into their current English equivalents: und in this way "frontera" was translated as "end" (p. 179f). It is in the latter interpretation that it is accepted here.

[19] Sahagun, p. 298. But in a later passage (p. 320) the breadth is given as 20 paces, which would multiply the figures just given by a factor of three or six, depending on the value of the pace.

of 200 feet similarly measured (D). Motolinia's figures, which he offers as an average value, are intermediate between these extremes and agree pei haps better with those of Sahagun than with Duran's: a breadth of 24 feet by a length (measured as before) of 120 feet. There is general agreement in setting the height of the side walls at between 1.5 estados (8 feet 4 inches: M, S, D) and 2 estados (11 feet: S, D).

The archeological evidence confirms the variation in dimension indicated by these discrepancies. Considering only the full length of the court and the width of alley, values run respectively from 97 feet to 226 feet (29.4 to ca. 69 meters) in length, with widths that range between ca. 12 and 41 feet (3.6 to 12.4 meters).[20]

Markers: The early chroniclers never fail to mention as one of the most distinctive features of the Mexican courts the paired stone rings *(tlachtemalacatl, tlatlachemalaca)*, like twin mill stones, set on tenons into the side walls at the middle of the court, about 1.5 estados (8 feet 4 inches) above the floor. Each bore a central hole just large enough for the passage of the ball (M, G, S, D). It is evident from the archeological remains that the rings were so placed that their plane faces were perpendicular both to the side walls and to the ground.

Not all of the courts excavated give evidence of having been provided with rings. In particular, in southern Mexico these markers are absent, and writers have seized on another feature, the paired niches set generally into the face of the end walls, as a local alternative to the rings. With the possible exception of the small court at Tula[21] the two features have not been found associated in the same court. Alternative explanations among those set forth by Caso, to the effect that they may have served as repositories for images of patron gods or for the equipment used in play, appear more likely.[22]

[20] For comparison with Maya figures, the few figures bearing upon the alley length and breadth are here presented. Excavation of the smaller community centers should do much to amplify these figures.

Length of alley	Average breadth of alley	No. of Courts
51—Above	9.3	2
41—50	8.6	2
31—40	—	—
21—30	5.7	2
10—20	3.6	1

While it is not my purpose to enter into detailed analysis of these data, it is well to point out that the largest courts are not restricted to any one area, though it may later prove that they may not be too far apart in time. The small number of excavated courts should be enough to warn the investigator against building too weighty a speculative structure upon them.

[21] Acosta, 1940.

[22] Caso, 1935, p. 12. Caso also considers the possibility that the niches may have served as goals or as astronomical markers. They are not usually set along the major axis of the court.

To those who were eye witness to the game, however, the rings and the play centered upon them formed one of its most spectacular characteristics, without strict parallel in Europe, and they lavished attention upon them. It is striking, therefore, to find Alvarado Tezozomoc, the scion of Aztec royalty, describing the court as having a hole in the center, larger than a bowling ball in diameter, called the *itzompan* (Seler translates this as "place of the skull"). When the court is divided in half, he continues, a triangle is drawn about the hole, which is termed the well of water. The details of play he mentions indicate that both hole and triangle function together in a manner identical with the paired rings described by other writers.

It would be easy to dismiss the central hole as a mere allegorical fiction, particularly since it is found in the Tezozomoc account in a description of the first, legendary game played by the migrant forefathers of the Tenochcas (Aztecs). However, both tense and clarity of detail urge that much of the description is based on personal observation and Tezozomoc, as we know, was in a good position to witness the game. It must be admitted that the ambiguity of his language does little to assist the reader to reach a conclusion.

Fortunately, the codices offer a measure of illumination on this point. Ball courts occur frequently on their pages, although not always in a form to be utilized. As an ideograph, the court is often only sketchily outlined, and so must be disregarded for present purposes. On the other hand, the more detailed delineations present features about which we would otherwise know nothing. Among the more elaborate representations are a number which fail to show the paired rings, even in courts in which a game is then in progress. Pictures of this class do not readily fall within restricted regions or chronological horizons.[23] The inter-

---

[23] Among the classifications of codices which have been consulted are those of Seler (especially 1902) and Lehmann, the latter to a lesser extent; the arrangement of Spence (pp. 378—381), which rests largely upon Seler; and Vaillant (pp. 291—4: Notes 17 for ch. 9 and 5 and 22 for ch. 11).

References to the figures cited are as follows: Cod. Magliabecchiano, XIII—3, fig. 68 (rings); Cod. Florentino, pl. 51, bk. 8; cf. Durán ch. 23, pl. 2 (rings); Cod. Borgia, pls. 21, 40, 42 (rings); pl. 35 (central hole ?); Cod. Fejérváry-Mayer, fol. 29 (side markers); Aubin Tonalamatl, pl. 19 (central hole); Cod. Nuttall, pls. 45, 80 (neither rings nor other paired markers); pl. 74 (rings and alley markers); Cod. Borbonicus, pls. 19, 27 (rings); Cod. Colombino, pl. 2 (central hole), pl. 11 (side markers ?); Bodleian 2858, pl. 10 (neither rings nor other paired markers), pl. 36 (central hole); and Historia Tolteca-Chichimeca, pl. 8, g (neither rings nor other paired markers). Less convincing examples also exist, but they will not be presented here.

Seler (1900), in commenting on the Aubin Tonalmatl (in which the court is merely a symbol of the game itself) calls attention to the variant form which it there presents (p. 19). He labels a round object outside the court as *ollamaloni* (i. e., the ball?) and the central hole, *tlachtemalacatl*, hastening to point out

pretative codices, drawn after the Conquest, do show only courts with paired rings. On the other hand, the Codex Borgia group, including the Codices Borgia, Fejérváry-Mayer, Bologna, Vaticanus B, and Laud, which, it is generally agreed, is of southern Mexican provenience, shows courts with and without rings, as well as courts with the central hole, and a similar range is manifest in the codices as yet unclassified. The same codex may, indeed, present several of the variants within its pages.

None of the courts thus far uncovered in the course of archeological excavations possesses the central hole; nor, for that matter, is there clear evidence for the existence of paired markers, such as are common in the Maya area. The lesser court at Tula does have "standard-bearers" that may have held markers,[24] although rings too may be present.[25] The top panel of a multiple pectoral from a tomb at Monte Albán,[26] which represents a ball game in progress, depicts paired serpent heads at the center of the side walls. Aside from this, there is not much direct evidence for the existence of paired markers, other than rings; but the negative testimony, in the absence to date of the latter in the southern courts, suggests that some sort of simple marker was used. The codices support this view in presenting several courts which lack any sort of paired marker.

In these courts (see fn. 23 above), the only markers perceptible are lines traced upon the ground along the major and minor axes of the court in such a manner as to divide it into equal quarters. Similar lines appear in most of the other court types as well, so that they can well be termed a constant feature of the ball court. According to Durán, the shorter line was drawn in black or green with a certain herb, so that it ran across the court between the two rings. He does not mention the longer line. Sahagun specifies that the dividing line was termed *tlecatl*; but neither he nor any other chronicler indicates the presence of the longitudinal marker. The codices, on the other hand, quite frequently show it, usually in conjunction with the transverse marker. Quite frequently, the resultant divisions are distinctively colored red, blue, yellow, and green. As Blom has already pointed out, the colors do not always appear in the same relative order,[27] even within the same page

however (p. 122) that the figure is incorrect, since there should be two rings. It may be added that the representation is otherwise variant in having the court divided into eight, rather than the customary two or four, sections.

Lovén (p. 524 and note 6) has already advanced the existence of the court with central hole, although in the example he adduces in support, that of the Codex Fejérváry-Mayer, the central object is clearly the ball (see Seler, 1901—2, vol. 1, fol. 29) and paired side markers are present.

[24] Acosta, 1940; 1941.
[25] Charnay, 1887, pp. 95—7; Acosta, 1940; 1941.
[26] Caso, 1932, p. 477.
[27] Blom, 1932, p. 513.

of a codex, so that it is difficult to consider them of directional significance. Rules of play, on the other hand, seem to bear upon the func-
tional character of the quartered court.[28]

Alley markers seem, in general, not to have extended into the Mexican
area to any degree. The Codex Nuttall, which is thought to have come
from southern Mexico does, however, in one instance (pl. 74) depict three
rosettes spaced evenly along the major axis of the court. They might
with reason be considered to represent alley markers, although none as
yet has been identified archeologically in this area.[29]

In the statement that walls were at times battlemented (M, D) or
bore stone images spaced along the top (D) there is a possible allusion
to still other forms of markers, analogous perhaps to those of the Maya
courts. They may, however, have had a predominantly decorative or
religious function. In addition, wild palms or redbean trees sometimes
crowned the walls (D).

Brief mention may be made of an essential feature of every court,
namely the image of the patron deity of the game (as well, we are told,
as that of the patron of the ball) which was placed in every court. Durán
states that the hole in each ring was surrounded by the face and form of
the god of the game; and the finding of many rings decorated by carved
motifs may bear him out. Likewise, adds the same author, there were upon
the walls of the court many pictures representing the "idols and demons
to whom that court was dedicated and to whom the players turned as
mediators in that sport" (p. 242 f). Mural paintings such as these must
have been at least in part alternative to sculptures in the round, for the
Spanish notation with regard to one deity states that he was depicted
in either form in the ball courts.[30] Indeed, all other writers mention
"idols," and devote several passages to the ceremonies involved in put-
ting them in place either in the lower, end walls (G, T, CS) or, possibly,
on the side walls (M) facing each other. In either position, the images
would have been located at the ends of one of the two lines traced on the
floor of the court. Since the religio-ceremonial features of the game will
be discussed below, it will suffice to state here that the court could not
be used until it had been dedicated and the images (and rings) had been
set in place.

[28] Occasionally a codex, delineating a game in progress, omits all lines of
division. This omission can, perhaps, be validly ignored as reflecting the opera-
tion of artistic selection. The same thing cannot as easily be said of the omission
of the rings in other pictures.

[29] Acosta and Moedano Koer (p. 37) do, indeed, believe that a modern game,
played in Oaxaca, represents a survival of an aboriginal form (see below). They
suggest that the bouncing of the ball on certain restricted spots of the court in
this game reflects a similar play on the alley markers of the Maya courts. To
some extent such an hypothesis must await support in the discovery of the
markers in Oaxaca.   [30] Cod. Magliabecchiano, XXX–3, pl. 33, verso.

Players *(ollamani)*: The popular hold of the ball game seems to have been well-nigh universal. In the interval between wars it was a favorite pastime of the emergent nobility; not only did they participate themselves but they retained professional players (M, S, D), whom they held in special esteem, bestowing upon them special insignia (D).[31] On the occasion of fair or market days, the nobility or their professionals demonstrated their skill; while at other times the public at large might also use the courts. There is no evidence that women took part at any time in the games.

Equipment: The professional players, as well as the members of the upper classes, seem to have owned a rubber ball as part of their paraphernalia (D), a condition that again presents a parallel to the Maya pattern. Nobles are said to have had page boys to whom they entrusted the ball between games (S).

When he went into the game, the player was clad only in a loincloth *(maxtlatl)*, over which a stiff leather girdle supported a skirt of tanned deerskin *(quezeuatl)*, covering the buttocks and thighs (M, S, D). Both hands, which might be employed as braces against the floor of the court during the game, were provided with gloves *(mayeumatl*: D, S).[32]

A comparison of the scenes depicted in the codices is illuminating. While in many cases the contestants are the gods or their human impersonators and retain the distinctive regalia even in the course of play, those who appear as mere mortals are stripped to the essential equipment already mentioned. Gloves, i. e. hand wrappings, are occasionally absent, but it is usual for one or both of the hands to be thus protected. Variations in respect to this feature are not regular enough to establish regional characteristics. On the other hand, knee pads are usual in the south and along the eastern lowlands, in this respect resembling the Maya. They are characteristically lacking in those codices which are attributable to tribes in the Valley of Mexico.

It might further be noted that Seler has often interpreted as the *quezeuatl*, or hip leather, a sash-like device held doubled in the hand of

[31] The fact that 16,000 rubber balls annually formed part of the royal tribute from southern Mexico (Codex Mendoza) underscores the association between the upper classes and the game (Cf. fn. 16 above).

[32] In addition to the players depicted in the codices listed in fn. 23 above, mention may be made of a player in action portrayed in the Codex Mendoza (p. 70, no. 7); of a figurine illustrated by Blom (fig. 9); and of several similar figurines reproduced by Ekholm (1946, pl. 1, c, d). The bas-relief from Tepatlaxco, Vera Cruz, has already been cited (fn. 18 in preceding chapter).

Finally, passing reference may be made to a clay figurine from the Tehuantepec region, now in the possession of Sr. Miguel Covarrubias. Dr. Gordon Ekholm, to whose courtesy I owe permission to mention it here, has shown me a photograph of the figurine, which is of the "Archaic" type. The player is represented as provided with girdle, a quilted glove on the left arm, and with a helmet complete with chin strap.

some players. However, the balls held by these and other players in the codices often emit smoke, suggesting that a pre-game ceremony is actually in progress. Spence has, indeed, linked the two, designating the problematical object as a copalbag.[33] While not necessarily subscribing to the specific identification of Spence, I believe his the more logical interpretation. In the Codex Borgia (pl. 4) several players in the end courts each bear a rodlike object on one hand and a smoking sphere in the other. That these objects do not function in the game proper is, however, indicated by a central figure, who strikes with his hip a ball that is larger than the globes of incense borne by the other players.

Officials: Bancroft states that a priest served as referee in case of disputes.[34] Some such official functioning as a score keeper or umpire, seems indicated, in view of the presence of similar dignitaries in northern Mexico. However, I have been unable to identify the original source of this statement, and so accept it only with reservations.

Wagers: Both the players and spectators commonly laid wagers on the outcome of the game, the stake varying with the status and wealth of the individual. Rulers might play for principalities or kingdoms, as when Axayacatl, the sixth ruler of Tenochtitlan, wagered his yearly income, together with several cities, against Xihuitlemoc's city, Xochimilco.[35] When the allies, Nezahualpilli of Texcoco and Montezuma II of Tenochtitlan, played to determine the authenticity of a prophecy, the former wagered the kingdom of Acolhua against a nominal stake of three turkeys.[36] Lesser nobles and chiefs played for jades and turquoises, jewelry of gold, for feather robes, mantles, articles of clothing and of panoply, for cocoa, cornfields, and houses, and for slaves and concubines. The gambling mania also drove the common people, though their means were less, and they wagered fields, crops, granaries, and houses; they sold their children into slavery to meet their bets or gambled their own persons (D, S, CS). Durán depicts the impoverished devotee, the professional gambler, centering his whole existence upon the game, while his family must beg for their bread.

These conditions, however, must not be regarded as pertaining exclusively to the ball game, for wagers were equally steep in the draughtlike game of *patolli* (G).

Teams: Usually the sides were equally matched, with two or three players on each team; but on occasion one or two players might compete against three (M). Codices sometimes show only one player on each side; and this was apparently the case when nobility played, as in the famous match between Axayacatl and Xihuitlemoc, cited above, and

[33] Spence, 1923, p. 97.
[34] Bancroft, 1886, p. 298.
[35] Torquemada, vol. 1, bk. 2, ch. 59, p. 180f.
[36] *Ibid*, ch. 77, p. 212.

in the games between professionals, whom the nobles took with them from town to town to pit against other champions.

In team play, the prevailing strategy was to place the best players in the alley, with the others in the end courts to return balls that would otherwise go dead there (D).

Play: We are told that the ball had to be struck with hip, buttock, or knee: to hit it with any other part of the body was to forfeit a point for the side of the offending player. Yet this was merely the courtly game, the ideal type of play. Even Duran, who devotes a passage to it, implies that there were other methods of hitting the ball, albeit less favored.[37] The matter is stated in simplest terms by a 16th century writer, Dr. Francisco Hérnández. "They drive the balls with various parts of the body," he observes, "and they are returned by those guarding the opposite goal, and it is not permitted to touch them with the hands. At times, by agreement of both sides, it is allowed to touch them only with the hips and only on the first, second, or third bounce."[38] It seems probable that beginners and less gifted players in general were subject to fewer restrictions on the parts of the body that could be used.

How the ball was put into play is not specified, but a serve that went bad was repeated (M). The ball might be struck as long as it was still bouncing (G), but it must be returned past the middle (transverse) line by a distance of at least two fingers to be good (D). Players seem to have remained in their own court, behind the transverse line, although some interchange of position seems to have taken place (M).[39] Each team defended one of the rings and a wall. Since the game was played for a total number of points agreed upon beforehand, and since only a rare stroke sent the ball through the ring, thereby winning the game at once (M, G, S, D), it is evident that the more usual method of scoring involved a play for the wall. Indeed, there were three ways of winning a point: the ball might be driven over the top of the opponents' goal wall, or merely bounced against it; it might be sent into the body of a competitor outside of the prescribed body area, so that he committed a body fault; or a shot might be so placed, for instance, in one of the side arms of the end-zone, that it went dead there before the other team could return it

[37] Martyr (Dec. 5, bk. 10, ch. 5, p. 469) in a passage that is otherwise anomalous, states that the Mexicans played with shoulders, elbows, head, and rarely with the hands, while they sometimes struck the ball with buttocks as well.

[38] Hérnández, p. 93 (translation mine). Aside from this passage, the text comprises chiefly an abridgment of similar descriptions in Gómara and others, whom he cites as his primary authorities.

[39] The pertinent sentence is somewhat obscure as to meaning: "Otros atravesaban y atenianse á la una parte y las otras á otra..." (Motolinia, 1903, p. 339).

(M, G, D). The object of play was thus not to gain ground, or to make chases, but to score (M, G, D).[40]

Each team appears to have been assigned one of the two rings as a goal. The contestant that sent the ball through the proper ring won the game o utright. By all tokens, the feat was a rare one, for the hole was so sma l that the ball could scarcely pass through. "A man, throwing it by h nd from close range," asserts Motolinia, "could not put it in once in one hundred tries, nor in two hundred." When a player so scored, a near panic ensued, for he was entitled to the cloaks of all the spectators,[41] who thereupon took to their heels, abusing him as a man bewitched. They were closely followed by some of his teammates, who sought to collect the cloaks that were forfeit. The remainder of his fellow players sang and danced in his honor, giving him a prize of feathers or loin cloths, perhaps from the total wagered, and heaping upon him the praise accorded the victor in a group duel or combat (D). He then made sacrifices to the image of the patron god of the game and to the ring through which the ball had passed (M).[42]

[40] The identity of the goal wall is of interest, since it bears upon the direction of play. It might with logic be argued that the end wall, *pared frontera*, served this purpose (see fn. 18 above), and analogies could be drawn with the function of the *frontón* (tennis) or *frontis (pelota vasca)* in Europe. Motolinia, indeed, is the most specific of those who denote the goal, and his statement might be interpreted to allude to the end walls: "los que la [i. e. the ball] echaban por cima de la pared de frente ó atoparen en la pared ganaban una raya . . ." (p. 338).

It must be admitted that the identification here proposed has the logical defect of introducing to the game two diametrical directions of play, one toward the end walls and the other toward the rings set in the side walls. These courses would, as a matter of fact, take the same direction as the two intersecting lines traced on the floor of the court. None of the texts consulted gives sanction for such an interpretation, nor does any specifically disprove it.

Alternative suggestions, however, which would view the side walls as the goal designated, run into difficulty in the physical dimensions of the court. In the area under consideration, alley width ranges from 11.8 to 40.6 feet (3.6–12.4 meters), a value well below the distance achieved with the rubber ball by players in other regions. To consider the side wall the goal would be to ensure a point at almost every stroke.

In truth, even this objection could be met. Each team had assigned to it as major goal one of the two rings. A limited part of the wall adjacent to the ring might then be regarded as a subsidiary goal: indeed the entire expanse of wall on that side, within the opponents' court, might serve this purpose. Such a proposition does, however, appear inherently less probable than that initially set forth.

Neither rings nor walls seem to have been absolutely essential to the game. In Durán's time, all the courts had been demolished, yet the game was maintained, though probably with modifications.

[41] Motolinia states that he was due only the mantles of those supporting the defeated team.

[42] A somewhat similar account is given by Alvarado Tezozomoc, who however substitutes the central hole for the ring.

Games might be played in silence, though players were in the habit of calling upon their supernatural helper, either to themselves or aloud (D). When one team was ahead, silence seems to have been forsaken, and the leading side would pour abuse on the heads of their hapless rivals (M, D).

The pace of play was intense, for the game demanded great agility and endurance. Tired players frequently miscalculated, receiving the heavy ball in the stomach; a blow which usually proved fatal. Even in the ordinary course of play, participants suffered great bruises upon the thighs and knees, which had to be lanced to draw off the blood (D).

Most of the early accounts hitherto cited upon Mexico either describe the ball game played in the Valley of Mexico, or else cannot be localized. It is accordingly of importance to compare the description given by Muñoz Camargo, a noble Tlaxcalan mestizo, who was born shortly after the Conquest and who, in his *Historia de Tlaxcala*, gives a brief sketch of the game as it was played in his native land.

> They had ball games of a very strange sort which they called the game of *Ulli*. It is a ball made of a certain milk which a tree called *Ulquahuitl* gives forth, which changes into strong fibers that bounce so much that there is nothing in this world to compare with it. The balls are like those of rope that are used in Spain and bounce so much that, if one did not see it, it would seem incredible. And, bouncing the ball on the ground, it rises more than three estados in the air. This ball is struck with the hips or buttocks, since it weighs so much that it could not be struck with the hands; and thus those who play with this ball have very broad leather girdles, made of chamois, for the hips and buttocks with which they play. They had ball courts in the Republic [i. e. Tlaxcala] dedicated to this pastime; the sons of nobles played for exercise, and they played for very steep stakes, clothing, gold, slaves, emblems, and they played for feather-work, and other riches. There were great wagers in this game; they were very solemn games of the Republic; no one played but great lords, and not the common people; they had representatives for this game.[43]

Aside from the restriction of the game to the nobility, which may well have taken root from Camargo's desire to establish the prerogatives of the class of which he was a member, there is no disparity between his account and those for the remainder of central and southern Mexico. Herrera likewise intimates royal prerogatives with respect to the game among the Mixtec of Oaxaca, stating that the "pope" could go out to play ball games at the royal establishment.[44] Of Michoacon, the same author merely assures us that they had the ball game, as in Mexico.[45]

Secular associations: It might be well to recapitulate the surroundings forming the secular context of the game. Major ball courts were located in the market places, and lesser ones in the suburbs. These were

[43] Muñoz Camargo, 1892, pp. 135–6 (translation mine).
[44] Herrera, Dec. 3, bk. 3, ch. 13, p. 99.
[45] *Ibid*, ch. 10, p. 94.

frequented, not only by those of high rank, but by anyone interested in the game. The ruler himself might participate and under such circumstances, we are told, music greeted the victor.[46] On festival days, the upper classes thronged the courts, pitting themselves or their professionals in public exhibitions of the greatest skill and dexterity. The walls "swarmed with people when there was a general game of the nobility, which was whenever the pursuit of war stopped, by reason of truces or for other cause, and gave them the opportunity."[47] The aggressive play underscored by taunts and jeers, the high stakes and personal risk, all emphasized the belligerent nature of the game. Here a player might lose wealth, a kingdom, his very freedom, life itself. A poor man who had staked his liberty might end up as a sacrifice to the gods (D). The story of the game played by Axayacatl, ruler of the Tenochcas, and Xihuitlemoc, chief of Xochimilco, alluded to previously, shows clearly how in the hands of the Aztecs, the ball game could become an adjunct of war. Axayacatl, desiring the death of his neighbor, invited him to play, and so taunted him that he could not refuse. Each put up a stake, some towns on the Lake against the city of Xochimilco, and entered into play. Xihuitlemoc won easily and the defeated Axayacatl saved face and wager only through the expedient of assassination.[48]

Ixtlilxochitl tells us that Topiltzin, Toltec king, seeing himself oppressed by three rivals, who encroached on his lands, sent them, among other precious jewels, a ball court the size of a medium room, made of four kinds of precious stones, together with a carbuncle to serve as ball. He then proposed that the four of them play, the winner to rule the others; and thus they would live in peace.[49]

The sportive side of the ball game was paramount in the eyes of the Spaniards, who tended to align it with tennis, with which it presented patent analogies, not only in the details of play, but in its courtly prestige as well. That they were in some measure right is suggested by the identity of the deity often cited as patron of the game: he was also the god of gaming, of feasting, and of pleasure. Yet other deities were likewise associated with the ball game, and other patrons have been put forward in whom no sportive character is manifest. Like all men, the early chroniclers saw the New World through the "glass of custom," which then as now distorted the image seen. In the ball game, we may suspect some distortion; we may even venture to bring some elements

---

[46] Torquemada, vol. 1, bk. 2, ch. 77, p. 212.

[47] Durán, p. 243 (translation mine).

[48] Torquemada, vol. 1, bk. 2, ch. 59, p. 180f. As the historian puts it, what irked Axayacatl was "not so much the income as the credit and standing as a player, on which he prided himself."

[49] Ixtlilxochitl, relac. quinta, p. 50. It is probably upon this authority that Vaillant states that Topiltzin (ruled 885–959) introduced the ball court (p. 55).

back into perspective; but we can never restore those details which that glass obscured from view.

Magico-religious associations: The player felt that his play was affected by the day sign under which he had been born and by the intervention of his protecting divinity (M, G, D), upon whom he called in the course of the game. The professional gambler, however, went further. The night before the game, he placed the ball in a clean plate and suspended his hip leathers and gloves from a pole. Squatting before them, he prayed to the natural forces and to the gods for success, burning incense and making offerings of food. During this time he fasted, and on the following morning he partook of the consecrated victuals (D). His chances of success might be further enhanced, if, in addition, he had inverted the metate and griddle within the house and placed the grinding roller in a corner.[50]

The deeply pervasive influence of Aztec religious ceremonial, suffused as it was through every aspect of daily life, made its presence felt here. The central symbol of the ball game, the court, was itself surrounded by emblems of divinity. "Each court," says Gómara, followed by Cervantes Salazar and Torquemada, "was like a temple, because they put two images of the god of the ball game on the lower walls;" "and for this reason," adds Motolinia, "they were destroyed."[51] The latter has left us a detailed description of the consecration of the court:

> When the court has been completed and plastered, at midnight on an auspicious day they put the heart in the court with certain witcheries,[52] and in the middle of the court and in the center of the walls, one and a half estados up on the inner side they set stones little smaller than millstones: each one had a tenon which went into the wall, by which it was supported: each one of these stones had in the center a hole through which the ball could barely pass. When this had been done, in the morning they decorated two idols[53] and put them on top of the walls of the *tlachco* in the middle, one

[50] Authority for the latter statement is Thompson, 1933, p. 235. I have been unable to discover the original source.

[51] It is interesting to observe that, while Motolinia and Gómara (together with some of the latter's plagiarists) agree in seeing an idolatrous connotation in the ball court, only the former cites this as the reason for its destruction by the Spaniards. Salazar, civil chronicler of Mexico (and, after him, Herrera) ascribe it to a desire on the part of the conquerors to protect the Indians from the very real dangers of play. The latter motivation is, to say the least, suspect. That the courts were destroyed, and very probably for the very reason adduced by Motolinia, is shown by the statement of Durán, in whose time the game was carried on without this adjunct. By the time of Clavigero, the game was gone from central Mexico and only lingered on, as it has to the present, in the north.

[52] See Codex Borgia, pl. 40, for an illustration of a similar sacrifice.

[53] Gómara states that they represented the god of the game (or court), in which he is followed by Cervantes Salazar. Torquemada (followed by Herrera), on the other hand, is of the opinion that only one image depicted this deity, the other representing the god of the ball. Further evidence as to the identity of the patron gods will be cited below.

facing the other,[54] and then they sang there before them and recited their chants, each god having his own chant or chants, and others went as messengers to the temples to inform the priests that they had made a ball court and fulfilled therein all the solemnities and ceremonies, that there remained nothing more to do but for a priest to go to bless and sanctify it. Several of those priests came, black as those who come from Hell, and took the ball and threw it four times against the court.[55]

And with this it was consecrated and they could play in it, which up to that time they could not do in any form; not even the proprietor of the court, who was always a lord, could play ball without first performing I know not what ceremonies and making offerings to the idol, so superstitious were they.[56]

The gods linked in one way or another with the ball game were many, a condition that in some degree may be said to reflect in the divine universe the mundane popularity which it enjoyed. In the more regular associations of particular deities or classes of supernaturals with the game, however, the symbolic identities which it may have borne for the Mexican people can be dimly perceived. These have received extensive comment by several authorities, and since they are material to the interpretation of the position held by the ball game among the Mexicans, it will be the subject of somewhat involved discussion here.

Of the great gods and their adjutants or variants, Huitzilopochtli and Painal, Tezcatlipoca, and Quetzalcoatl and Xolotl are sometimes depicted in the ball court. Fertility deities that likewise are shown include Xipe Totec, Centeotl, Coatlicue, Xochiquetzal, and Xochipilli, in addition to such minor figures as Five Lizard and Ten Lizard. Tlaloc, the rain god, makes but a rare appearance as a player. No other deity appears with any frequency in the court, and it remains to be seen how necessary were the bonds between those just named and the ball game.[57]

Some of the principal concepts surrounding the ball game appear in a migration legend of the Aztec peoples recounted by Tezozomoc[58] and Veytia.[59] When the errant tribes reached Coatepec, in Otomi country,

[54] Gómara, together with the authors who have followed him, states that the images were placed in the two lower walls. Logically, this might allude either to the benches or to the end walls; but since his previous descriptions had had reference only to the higher side-walls and the lower *paredes fronteras,* which I have interpreted as designating the end-walls, it seems preferable to consider the images as having been set in the middle of the end-walls, facing each other. On the other hand, some variation might be expected: the remains of house structure on the ranges of some courts which have been excavated suggest that the images might be laterally placed, and a sculptured stone jaguar was actually set on the range of the lesser court at Tula (Acosta, 1940).

[55] Motolinia, 1903, p. 337f, (footnotes mine).

[56] Gómara, 1940, p. 216.

[57] Classification of the gods follows Vaillant (table X), while their attributes are in the main derived from Seler (1908, 1923, and his commentaries on the various codices) and from Spence *(passim)*.

[58] Ch. 2, pp. 227–9.

[59] Vol. 1, bk. 2, ch. 13, pp. 296–8.

their patron deity and war god, Huitzilopochtli, decided to reveal to them what the promised land would be like.[60] When they had built his temple and their villages, he accordingly bade them construct a ball court, *teotlachco*, with a hole, the "well of water," in the center. When this was done, and they had planted the crops he commanded, there came forth from the hole a stream of water to irrigate their fields.[61] The abundance in this place made many people loath to leave and follow the god, and their dissatisfaction found a ringleader in his sister, Coyol-xauhqui.[62] One night, therefore, Huitzilopochtli slew her in the central hole of the court, beheading her and taking out her heart; after which he served her followers in the same way.[63] Then he broke the conduit and transformed the court into a lake from which the water drained away; and birds, fish, trees, and plants vanished like smoke, leaving the land desolate and unattractive.

So much for the legend. Now, in Sahagun's description of the great temple of Tenochtitlan, dedicated to Huitzilopochtli and Tlaloc, mention is made of two ball courts within the temple compound, designated respectively *tezcatlachco* ("mirror ball court") and *teotlachco* ("divine ball court"). Of the former, it is only known that it was located between the temple bases, and that captives were slain therein "in the ruling sign of *omácatl*."[64] The reference appears to be, not to the deity of that name, but to the date, Two Reed, within the *tonalpohualli*, or 260-day ritual cycle. Since that day was also the initial day of each 52 year cycle, it is probably in that connection that the captives were slain.[65]

[60] In another connection, Coatepec is the scene of the parthenogenic birth of Huitzilopochtli to the earth goddess, Coatlicue, and the place where he subsequently defeated and slew his four hundred brothers in her behalf.

[61] In both the *Historia de los Mexicanos por sus Pinturas*, ch. 11, and the *Codex Ramirez*, it is stated that Coatepec stood near the town of Tula. As will be shown subsequently, the ball court there was distinctive of that town. Does the *teotlachco* appear in the legend as a symbol of the higher civilization upon which the Aztecs were now impinging? It seems probable. The latter account has Huitzilopochtli bring plenty upon the land by instructing his priests to deflect the course of a river (see Radin, 1920, pp. 58f., 72–4).

[62] Once again there is a merging of the origin myth of Huitzilopochtli and the legendary migration; for leader of the matricidal siblings who sought the death of Coatlicue and first to be slain instead was this selfsame sister. Moreover, her Aztec supporters in the legend in one passage receive the same name as that borne collectively by the four hundred brothers of the origin myth.

[63] Seler (1908, p. 326) points out that, just as the ball court is called for the god, *itlach*, his ball court, so the central hole bears the name *itzompan*, his place of skulls. Cf. the name of the skull rack, *tzompantli*, shown in the Codex Florentino (Estampa XI) and adjacent to the ball court in the great temple compound of Huitzilopochtli and Tlaloc.

[64] Sahagun, vol. 1, bk. 2, pp. 215, 223. Chavero (p. 791) locates the two courts more specifically within the compound.

[65] See Vaillant, pp. 187–200, for a convenient description of the Mexican calendrical system.

In the second court, the *teotlachco*, there may be recognized the counterpart of the court of the migration legend. Situated in the middle of the patio, it figured prominently in the festival of Panquetzaliztli, in the fifteenth month of the solar calendar, which was dedicated to Huitzilopochtli. In the ceremony enacted about the court, described by Sahagum in three somewhat variant passages, there is perhaps a partial recapitulation of the legend. At this point, many preliminaries had brought the festival toward a climax by the nineteenth day. At dawn (of the next day ?) a priest, clad in the vestments of Quetzalcoatl, descended the great temple of Huitzilopochtli bearing a wooden image of Painal, the war god's vicar or messenger. He was preceded by a mace bearer with the torquoise-covered serpent, the special weapon of Huitzilopochtli, and was accompanied by the captives to be sacrificed. When they reached the *teotlachco* four captives were slain, two each in honor of the gods, Amápan and Oappátzan, whom they represented and whose statues stood by the ball court. Their corpses were dragged about the court until their blood had stained the entire floor, after which Painal took his way, running through the various quarters of the city.[66] The remainder of the ceremony is not relevant to the present discussion.

The suspicion is evoked that the two gods, Amápan and Oappátzan, must be closely linked to the ball game; that, indeed, they may be the very patrons of the ball and of the game (or court) whose images were set upon the walls of the *tlachco*. That they are variant versions of the same god seems indicated by passages in Sahagun which designate the victims as *amapanme* and the gods collectively as *Amapantzitzin*. The name seems basically to comprise the roots *amatl*, paper, and the locative, *pan;* but efforts to identify some local deity with this name are so far unavailing.[67]

The second great divinity, Tezcatlipoca, possessed of occult powers and sometimes identified with the moon, appears in the ball court as a contestant.[68] Thus the Codex Borgia depicts the red Tezcatlipoca, a manifestation of the fertility deity, Xipe Totec, engaged in play against his black counterpart, while a human sacrifice lies in the middle of the court.[69]

[66] Sahagun; (Panquetzaliztli) vol. 1, bk. 2, ch. 15, p. 105f; ch. 34, p. 196; append., p. 215f. Location of the two courts: vol. 1, bk. 2, append., pp. 223, 224.

[67] I have distinguished company here, for Spence, in describing the ceremony, merely alludes to "the god Oappatzan," and goes no further (p. 71). It would be loosely speculative indeed to hazard a connection between Quetzalcoatl, as the preceptor of writing to mankind, and the deities in question. As will appear, there are sounder grounds upon which to establish a relation between him and the ball game.

[68] It is perhaps from his lunar identity that Chavero (p. 791) has been led to conclude that the *tezcatlachco* in the great temple compound of Tenochtitlan represented the movements of the moon — a conclusion not otherwise supported.

[69] Seler, 1906, pl. 40. Serpent heads which adorn the rings have led Blom (p. 499) to assign this court to Quetzalcoatl.

More frequently, Tezcatlipoca appears in the role of the arch foe of the culture hero, Quetzalcoatl. Tollan (Tula), the mythical capital of the latter, was noted for its "sorcery ball court,"[70] and there Tezcatlipoca engaged the patron god in play. In the middle of the game, the visitor changed himself into a tiger, terrifying the spectators, who took flight, only to fall into a ravine.[71] A subsequent episode in the same cycle, when Quetzalcoatl is in full flight before the machinations of the sorceror and his fellows, betrays a deeper nexus between the god and the game. Even driven as he was, the culture hero found time to work his wonders on the lands through which he passed; and among them, the ball court, made of squared stones, with the dividing line, *tlécatl*, across the middle. Along that line the earth was deeply cleft.[72]

Quetzalcoatl thus appears as a prominent participant in the ball game. His skill in play is praised. In the Codex Borgia he competes with Youaltecutli in a court the central goal of which seems to be the body of Tonacatecutli, the moon.[73] The Codex Borbonicus depicts him in conjunction with the court in what may be a ceremony.[74] The deities represented, Ixlilton (god of the dance) and Centeotl (maize god) at one end, and Quetzalcoatl and Cihuacoatl (an earth goddess) at the other, are those prominent in the Tecuilhuitontli, the ceremony of the seventh month, for rain and salt.[75] These instances are not intended to be exhaustive. Finally, it might be remarked that even in the Panquetzaliztli rite, which honors Huitzilopochtli, it is Quezalcoatl who bears Painal down to the sacred court.

Yet perhaps more than anything else, it is through his twin, Xolotl, that the god is most firmly linked to the ball game. For Xolotl is presented as patron of the game, in which he also appears as a participant. Seler states that there is a direct relationship between this god of twins or pairs and the duality implicit in competition.[76] In the course of the Atamalqualiztli, a fast and festival which occurred every eight years, a song was sung of which the ninth stanza runs:

> Old Xolotl plays ball, plays ball,
> In the sorceror's ball court he plays
> Lord of the land of the precious jade.[77]

[70] See Preuss and Menghin, pl. 8, g, for this court, as depicted in the Historia Tolteca-Chichimeca.

[71] Mendieta, bk. 2, ch. 5, p. 82. In other versions of this legend, e. g. Sahagun's, Tezcatlipoca achieves the same destruction by different means.

[72] Sahagun, vol. 1, bk. 3, ch. 14, p. 281.

[73] P. 35.

[74] P. 27.

[75] Seler, 1923, pp. 116, 118.

[76] Seler, 1900, p. 110.

[77] Sahagun, vol. 5, Los Cantares a los dioses, XIV, p. 136 (translation mine).

Whether the ball court is the sorcery ball court at Tollan need not be discussed here. The Codex Magliabecchiano says that Xolotl was the deity that appeared in the court, and adds that the likenesses were either painted or in the round, and states that Quetzalcoatl also appeared there.[78] There is no assurance that the two appeared together, but the references to a god of the ball and god of the game (or court) suggest that this may have been the case. Only so might some significance be seen in the fact that Amápan and Oappátzan were close enough to be designated by the name of one of them; but even so no direct evidence indicated that Xolotl was ever subsumed together with Quetzalcoatl in the latter's name.

Quetzalcoatl's connection with the ball game (and Xolotl's role may perhaps derive from it) seems adequately described in terms of his character of culture hero, preceptor of mankind.

The number of fertility deities associated with the ball game cannot be explained simply in terms of a projection of human pursuits. Many of them appear only infrequently, and solely as participants, but Xochipilli and Xochiquetzal, who rule over sensual gratification, are both sometimes presented as patrons of the game. Xochipilli, whose special sphere is feasting and sports, makes his appearance in the court, as Centeotl, the young maize god, or in his own variant forms of Macuilxochitl or Xochipilli. Durán's statement that the rings of the court bore the image of the god of the game, who "had a face in the form of a monkey's," and "whose festival was celebrated once a year,"[79] may refer to Xochipilli, whose day name was Eleven Monkey. Xochiquetzal, goddess of gaming and lust, is depicted as presiding over the game in both the Aubin[80] and Borbonicus[81] Tonalamatls. There can be very little doubt that these two deities denote by their patronage the sportive side of play.

Tlaloc is shown in the Codex Borgia in the garb of the ball player.[82]

Finally, consideration must be given to some of the symbolic values postulated by Seler for the ball game. Primary among them was a relation between the path of the ball in play and the movements of sun and moon; yet here Seler himself found it difficult to reconcile the prevailing north-south orientation of the then known archeological courts with the path of those two bodies.[83] In pursuit of the same line of reasoning, Seler adduced such representations as Codex Borgia, pl. 35, in which Quetzalcoatl plays against Youaltecutli in a court the central goal of which appears to be a figure identified as the moon god, Tonacatecutli; as well as the Codex Colombino, pl. 11, in which the lords of night and day contest the game. Frequently, however, he was led to

[78] XIII–3, pl. 33.
[79] Durán, 1867–90, p. 243.
[80] Seler, 1900, pl. 19.
[81] Hamy, pl. 19.
[82] Seler, 1906, pl. 7.
[83] Seler, 1908, p. 14f.

speak only in terms of the astral attributes of the deities participating in the game, which added little support to his thesis.

Closely bound to the foregoing hypothesis was an identification in imagery of the court itself with the earth.[84] Thus the quartered courts of the codices were identified with the four directions; a statement that has already been justly criticized by Blom.[85] Of the five earth goddesses, it is the kinkajou, *cuetlachtli*, that represents the center of the world.[86]

While many of the associations discussed above can, indeed, be explained in terms of the symbolism advanced by Seler, there is no objective proof that this was truly the *Mexican* configuration. Though Tezcatlipoca does make his appearance, and may at times partake of a lunar identity, the sun appears virtually unrepresented in the court. Of the courts now excavated, those in the north do indeed manifest an east-west orientation, but those in the southern areas are laid out on a north-south axis; and in general they reflect the bearings of associated structures.[87] Solar hypotheses were enormously popular at the time of Seler's *floruit*, and the fate of many of the theories then advanced induces double caution in accepting this one. At present there appears little explicit basis for his view, though it is only fair to say that Seler, with his vast knowledge of Aztec religion and ritual, may well have anticipated a full documentation of the facts supporting his thesis.[88]

It now seems feasible to assess the more important representative values that the ball game may have held for the Mexicans. In the legend relating to the fruitfulness of Coatepec there has been seen an allusion to a fundamental link between the *tlachco* and water, a nexus that gains support from the Codex Colombino (see fn. 23 above). Yet there is a good probability that the court may merely represent the adjacent town of Tula: in which case it may be regarded as emblematic, not of the primal fecundity of nature, but of god-taught and man-made improvement of the soil. In brief, the *teotlachco* may symbolize the high culture of the region the tribes were then entering.

---

[84] Seler, 1923, pp. 47-9.

[85] Blom, 1932, p. 513.

[86] Seler, 1923, p. 86f. Mention might be made here of another natural phenomenon, a constellation, which bears the name of the ball court. This is the *citlallachtli*, literally "star ball court," given originally by Sahagun, vol. 2, bk. 7, and discussed briefly by Seler, 1904, pp. 356-7.

[87] A measure of support for Seler's contention derives from the Spanish-Zapotec dictionary of Córdova (p. 224):

Iuego de pelota de Indios el lugar. Queye. 1. quiye. el que esta a oriente, y al poniente, quèyetòya. s. los puestos de cada vno.

Here the goals, probably the ends of the court, in accordance with general terminology, are located east-west.

[88] Seler's point of view is best presented in 1908, *passim*, upon which his later papers rest. See also 1923 and his commentaries on various codices.

If this is so, it may indicate why the ceremonial recapitulation of the legend is enacted at the Panquetzaliztli, during the winter solstice, at which time no ritual appeal seems to have been made for rain. It may also explain the presence of Quetzalcoatl, in proxy, at this portion of the festival.

Candidly, it must be admitted that other constructions, perhaps equally acceptable, may be, and indeed have been, put upon the legend and festival.[89] The delineation of Tlaloc as ball player in the Codex Borgia would accord with these views, which find a real association between the ball game and crop growth.

Finally, some basic concern with fruitfulness is, indeed, implicit in the performance of ceremonies in a ball court during the festival of Tecuilhuitontli, as well as in the appearance of fertility deities in the codices, likewise in conjunction with the court.

There is yet another connotation with which the game may have been invested, and here again Seler has been the first to discern it: "The ball game is quite properly the expression of duality, as well as of antagonism [Gegensätzlichkeit]."[90] In this sense, the game may be employed as a graphic abstraction of relationship, and in particular of polarity. This symbolic value may, in the end, turn out to be an explanation for the manifold occurrence of the ball game in Mexican art.

The game, in its intensely competitive character, may well become symbolic of warfare, and, through it, of the human sacrifice which becomes its objective. Huitzilopochtli overcomes his hostile sister in the court and slays her there. In the sorcery ball court of Tollan, Tezcatlipoca dramatizes his aggression against Quetzalcoatl. In the Totonac site of Tajin, as at the Mexican period portions of Chichen Itzá in Yucatan, ball-court panels bear processions which lead to the central sacrifice of a player. At the former site, the participants are armed for war, at the latter, they are not; though the difference is less than at first appears, since warrior processions appear in other associations on the panels of Chichen Itzá ball courts. Finally, the Codex Nuttall depicts a court within which two figures in war dress sit facing each other, with their weapons between them, apparently concluding a treaty.[91]

When one recalls the concern that was felt throughout Middle America for the proper conditions for agriculture, and the consequent preoccupation with fertility rites, there is no reason for surprise in the fact that the ball game itself became involved in the iconography of growth and

[89] See especially Seler, 1908, pp. 325–6 and E. S. Spinden, 1933, p. 247f. Neither of these authors relates legend and festival. The latter, it may be added, has presented a detailed and stimulating analysis of the symbolism of the ball court, with which I cannot always agree.

[90] Seler, 1923, p. 116.

[91] Nuttall, 1902, pl. 80 and p. 25.

ceremonialism. Human sacrifice, explicable in general terms as a measure to promote the favor of the gods, was especially directed toward ensuring fruitfulness. Finally warfare itself, as it grew to be the principal agency for securing the large number of victims demanded, likewise became subordinated to the central need. With them, the lesser institution of the ball game may be thought to have been drawn into the structure of ceremonialism.

Yet it is easy to go too far in this direction, to ignore the appeal, direct and uncomplicated, which the game made through its sportive qualities. That this fundamental value did not go unformulated is clearly indicated by the patronage of the gods Xochipilli and Xochiquetzal, who are sometimes shown presiding over the court.

There thus emerges a manifold significance which the ball game may be said to have possessed for the Mexicans. It shines at times with the reflected prestige of a higher civilization. It may become the image of opposed and contending forces, of warfare, and of death through sacrifice; and in a derivative sense it may thus be drawn into ceremonials revolving about propitiation of the gods. Finally, in a secular aspect, it may be regarded as sport.

Relationship with other ball games: The statement by Beals and Carrasco that "Ball players with clubs, playing in an 'I' – shaped court, are also shown in a mural recently discovered at Teotihuacan," suggests a variant form of the rubber-ball game. However, Acosta and Moedano Koer, who reproduce the mural in question,[92] do not show the court. Until it has been fully published, therefore, it would be best to leave the question in abeyance.

Molina's dictionary gives the following Nahuatl terms for ball games and the court:

Iuego de pelota con la mano. nematotopeuiliztli.
Iuego de pelota con las nalgas. ollamaliztli.
Iuego de pelota assi el lugar. tlachtli. ollamaloyan.
Iuego de pelota con la rodilla. netetemiuiliztli.[93]

It will be seen that only the game played with the buttocks *(nalgas)* contains the root for rubber, *olli*, and that the same root is present in a variant name for the ball court but is absent from the native terms for the games played with hand *(mano)* and knee *(rodilla)*. These facts justify the conclusion that the latter games did not employ a rubber ball and were not fundamentally linked with the court.

Further to the south, the Zapotec dictionary of Córdova gives additional information:

Iugar ala pelota de los yndios con las nalgas. Tiquija làchi.
Iuego assi. Quelacoqunalàchi.

[92] 1946, p. 374.   [93] Molina, 1880, p. 72.

Iugar a la pelota nuestra con la mano. Tigàapayapìtipi.
Iuego assi. Quela cogaapapitìpi.
Iuego de pelota de Indios el lugar, Quèye...[94]
Pelota antigua de los Indios para su juego. Làchi.
Pelota de las nuestras para jugar. Pitìpi.[95]

The lines are clearly drawn between the Indian game, played with the hips and using the ball, *làchi*, and the Spanish game, using the hand and the ball known as *pitìpi*. I have thus far been unsuccessful in determining the qualities of the balls described by these terms.

Other southern Mexican languages do not clarify the point. The Zoque vocabulary of 1733 gives only:

> *Jugar à la pelota*: coppa pecspa.
> *Jugar en general*: sipa.[96]

On the other hand, Tarascan again distinguishes clearly between the games mentioned in the Molina dictionary for Nahuatl:

Iuego de plazer. chanaqua.
Iuego de pelota con la mano. apantzequa chanaqua.
Iugar a la pelota con la mano. apantzeti.
Iugador assi. apantzeti.
Iuego de pelota con las nalgas. taranduqua chanaqua.
Iugar a la pelota con las nalgas. taranduni.[97]
Iugador tal. taranduti.[98]
Iuego de pelota con la rodilla. taranduqua hurincxtaqua.[99]
Pelota como quiera. xepandequa. apátzequa.
Pelota para jugar al batey. taranduqua.
Pelota de viento. apantzequa tariata hatziracata.[100]
Batel juego de pelota con las nalgas. taranduquaro querehtaro.[101]
Querehta, lugar do juegan a la pelota.[102]

Of the games mentioned, that using the hands is distinct from the others, and the ball employed is denoted only by a general term. The games utilizing buttocks and knee may be distinct: on the other hand, they use the same ball and may represent two methods of striking the ball in the same game. The ball court belongs properly to the game of hip ball. One is led to suspect from the complex descriptive name for the inflated ball that it is intrusive here. While the ball, *taranduqua*, used in hip ball is doubtless of rubber, my efforts to determine this from the name itself has thus far been unavailing.

On the evidence of vocabularies from various points within the Maya and Mexican areas, ball games other than hip ball were widespread throughout those areas shortly after the Conquest; and there is little

---

[94] Cordova, 1942, p. 224 (see also note 87).
[95] *Ibid*, p. 308.   [96] Vocabulario, p. 156.
[97] Gilberti, 1901, p. 372. [98] *Ibid*, p. 373.
[99] *Ibid*, p. 372.   [100] *Ibid*, p. 434.
[101] *Ibid*, p. 222.   [102] *Ibid*, p. 98.

doubt that most if not all of them were aboriginal in character. Prominent among them was hand ball, perhaps to be equated with the circle game of South America.

In Xoxocotlán, Oaxaca, there is a hand-ball game known locally as "*pelota mixteca*" that is still played by the mestizos and fullbloods. Acosta and Moedano Koer seem to consider it a modern survival of an indigenous form.[103] Through the courtesy of Dr. Gordon F. Ekholm, I have been able to examine equipment and a rule book (Pérez Bazán and Manterola) in his possession, and to include brief comments here.

In the light of the preceding discussion a good deal of interest surrounds a ball game described for 18th century Mexico by a native-born Guatemalteco, the Jesuit, Rafael Landívar.[104]

> Nothing, however, provides a more amazing spectacle than a large company of Indians given to play. They first gather a thick gum,[105] discharged by a tree, which gets its name from its elastic properties and by rolling it together form a large ball which freely bounces high into the air. The crowd then forms a large circle into which the large ball is first tossed and it is not permitted for anyone to touch it with his hands when once it has been thrown, but rather he must hit it with his hips, or elbows, or with his shoulders, or knees. Then as soon as the ball is tossed into the middle of the field, the whole crowd excitedly bounds over the plain darting this way and that. One hits the rubber ball with his elbow another drives it back with his hip, one thrusts his head in its way as it comes down, another with his knee quickly sends it back again into the sky or darting back and forth strikes it with one hip and then with the other. But if at any time the ball should alight on the broad surface of the ground the grounded ball must be retrieved with the elbow or the knees and lifted from the level plain into the air. For this reason you will see the Indians at this point of the game rolling all over the ground until they have raised the fallen ball with their elbows or knees. But if someone should venture to strike the ball with his hands while it is in the air and carelessly disregard the strict rule, he is reprimanded and suffers the loss of the game.[106]

Here, then, is what seems to be an eyewitness account of a game combining features that in South America are part of two discrete games: the initial formation and individual scoring of the circle game and the movement mode of striking, and hand fault that regularly accompany the competitive variant. Perhaps some of the former traits are more apparent than real. Landívar's account also combines methods of striking the ball that are nominally distinct in the Mexican and Maya areas. The most plausible explanation is that the game he describes is nothing less than a survival of the generalized practice bouts (cf. notes 37 and 38 above) underlying the formal competitive version. By the time he

---

[103] 1946, p. 366.

[104] Landívar, pp. 305–6.

[105] (Note 3 in original) "This gum, called *ule*, had extraordinary elasticity."

[106] (Note 4 in original) "This game is played today only among the Nayaritas, Tarahumaras, and some other northern tribes."

wrote, the courts had long since been demolished, with effects that were apparent even in the time of Durán. It is of course possible that further modifications may have arisen from the amalgamation of several native games and even from the incorporation of features from European cognates. On the other hand, the note which points to the survival of similar ball games among the tribes of northern Mexico may be discounted, since it patently echoes an almost identical statement by a fellow Jesuit, and fellow exile in Italy, Abbot Clavigero.

The Zapotec dictionary of Córdova indicates clearly that a Spanish ball game was introduced early in post-Conquest times in the region of Oaxaca and that it had become known to the Indians. "*Pelota mixteca*" in all probability bears strong traces of that game. In particular, the use of a wool-stuffed leather ball as an alternative to the solid rubber ball, the protection of the hand with a leather gauntlet sometimes reinforced by a studding of nail heads, the lay-out of the court and the appearance of what appear to be chases in play, and the method of scoring, proclaim European origin. Nonetheless, aboriginal traits may also be retained. Acosta and Moedano Koer have indeed pointed to an analogy between the level disk on which the server bounces the ball in service and the alley markers of the Maya courts.[107]

A game very much like *pelota mixteca* has been reported by Beals[108] for the modern Cáhita and will be considered below. The same explanation that has been offered for the Oaxacan game would probably be valid here as well. What appears to be a very similar game, known simply as *pelota*, is described from the Ecuadorean highlands by Parsons.[109] Its appearance in a place so distant from the other modern hand-ball games, taken together with the resemblances in equipment which point to a Spanish source, are cogent arguments for the view that all three examples represent in their essentials a European importation, rather than an indigenous development.

Accordingly, these games as they exist today cannot be received in evidence of the former use of the rubber ball in a hand-ball version of the usual game. The vocabularies which have been cited serve to confirm the distinctiveness of the hip-ball game within south and central Mexico and to link the ball court to it in an almost exclusive manner.

Relation between the Mexican and Maya Areas

Formerly, it had been a matter of common belief, amounting almost to dogma, that the rubber-ball game was a Mexican development introduced into the Maya area only in the course of the Toltec invasion

[107] *Ibid*, pp. 37 f.
[108] Beals, 1943.
[109] Parsons, 1945, p. 53.

(Thompson's Mexican Period). In 1932 Blom, in an incisive paper, thoroughly demolished this tenet. On linguistic grounds, he states:

> We note that the Maya called a round thing UOLLIC and it is most likely that the Aztec used the similar word, OLOLTIC, from which they derived OLLI to indicate rubber.[110] Maya traders brought their round balls of rubber to the Toltec-Aztec. The Maya word UOLLIC represents the form, whereas the Aztec use this word not only for the form but also for the material, and went still further by using the word OLLI, *rubber*, as part of the words which refer to the game played with the rubber ball.[111] From OLLI the conquerors got their name for rubber, which is HULE.
>
> Rubber grows chiefly along the Gulf coast of Mexico and in Yucatán, as well as on the tropical part of the Pacific coast. *It does not grow* in the country of the Toltec-Aztec. Rubber was brought to them by trade, and it would be just as natural for them to name it after the Maya word as it was for the conquerors to name rubber after the Nahua word.[112]

Having thus effectively reversed the cultural flow, Blom proceeds to substantiate his view by noting the many examples of Old Empire sites of which ball courts form a component, and comparing them with the paucity of courts, and those of relatively late date, within the Toltec-Aztec area. It was only in the time of the Toltec invasion, in his belief, that the indigenous Maya courts were replaced by the Mexican court with vertical walls and fixed stone rings.

Since that time, the discovery of ball courts of early date at the Hohokam site of Snaketown in Arizona has made it apparent that some simpler type of court must have been widespread throughout Mexico, perhaps long before the evolution of the complex courts of archeology.[113] The legend of Topiltzin, the ninth Toltec king, recounted by Ixtlilxochitl, and cited above, is interpreted by Vaillant as indicating the introduction of the ball court to those people in the period 923–47 A. D.[114] There is little doubt that the game itself, together with some form of court, had long since been introduced from the regions, possibly Maya, to the south. Indeed, the diffusion of the ball game throughout Middle America must

---

[110] Cf. the Zapotec (Córdova, p. 371): Redondo como bola o botija. Lòla, nàlòla, pel lòlo. The root faintly suggests a metathetic inversion of the Maya, uolol, which likewise designates a round object. In the form, pelòlo, it becomes an alternate for the verb, agent noun, and subject noun referring to the Spanish hand-ball game.

[111] The force of the latter argument is considerably diminished by evidence presented in the course of the present paper that many peoples designated the game by a name containing the root for ball, which in turn often resolves itself into the morpheme for rubber.

[112] Blom, 1932, p. 495f (footnotes mine).

[113] Thus Corbett (p. 55) postulates a northward diffusion of the game from the Maya region up the west coast of Mexico and thence to the Hohokam, reserving for a second, separate, movement its introduction, again from the Maya area, into the central Mexican and Totonac zones.

[114] Vaillant, 1944, p. 55 and Table V.

have been largely achieved by the end of the Formative period.[115] Its dissemination in northern Mexico and the southwestern United States, on the other hand, appears to have been somewhat later.

Northern Mexico and the Southern United States

Evid ınce now at hand for northern Mexico suggests a major extension of the rubber-ball game up the tierra caliente of either coast and in the flanking sierras, with little penetrations among the nomadic hunters of the great, arid North Mexican Interior Plateau.[116] For none of these areas are the data fully satisfactory, especially in those instances in which argument for absence must be made from the silence of all sources; and archeological surveys must accordingly be expected to amplify considerably the distributions offered here.

At the base of the interior plateau lies the area, comprising principally the present State of Querétaro, known as the Northeast Central Plateau. In aboriginal times it formed part of the homeland of the Otomí, to whom much of the archeological material in the state may justifiably be attributed. That they were subject to strong influences from the Valley of Mexico is well known; Vaillant indicates that Otomí tribes were forced out of the Lake Xaltocan region of the Valley itself in the 14th century A. D.[117] That the northward migration of the Otomí may have continued as a result of the displacements ensuing upon the Spanish conquest, and that the ball game may have been carried along, is suggested by a 16th century *relación*. According to this account, when Jilotepec, which lies some fifty miles northwest of Mexico City, fell to the Spaniards, the Otomí of the subject province of Nopal moved northward into the land of the "Chichimecs," with whom their leader had long carried on trade. There they founded a town in a ravine near the present city of Querétaro; and from a fancied resemblance in its situation, with low cliffs surrounding it, the leader gave it the Otomí name, *mexei*, ball court, for the game was a favorite of his. The name was subsequently transferred to the settlement of Querétaro.[118]

---

[115] Thompson (1943b, 1945) divides Maya history into four stages: Formative period (prior to 300 A. D.); Initial Series period (325–900 A. D.); Mexican period (987–1204 A. D.); and Mexican Absorption period (1204–1540 A. D.). The dates follow the Goodman-Thompson correlation.

[116] See Kroeber, 1939, Maps 1 A and 6, for the tribal distributions and corresponding cultural groupings for northern Mexico.

[117] Viallant, 1944, p. 75.

[118] Basauri (vol. III, pp. 274, 276–7) paraphrasing an account by Francisco Ramos de Cárdenas dated 1582. The present-day name for the city is the Tarascan word for ball court. Blom (1932, p. 497, note 14) gives an Otomí name for the ball court that cannot be said to equate with that of Cárdenas: "'Ndam-xey — lugar en el que se juega la pelota, o el major juego de pelota.'" Neve

Surveys within the modern state have revealed at least two sites which contain ball courts. The sites, Toluquilla and Ranas, are believed by Noguera to have been occupied coevally by members of the same cultural group. Ball courts appear to have been a prominent feature here for Toluquilla has two, and Ranas five of them. "They consist," says Noguera, "of two parallel walls with step *(escalón)* or sloping platform which runs along the whole inner face [of each]."[119]

Little enough, indeed, can be recovered to tell us how the Otomi played ball; the identification of their game with the type hitherto described rests only upon the analogies of court and rubber ball, and upon its proximity to the central Mexican area. The source of the rubber used is suggested by Altamirano, who states that certain species of *guayule*, known under the local name of *tatanini*, were utilized in his day by the country youths of Querétaro as a source of rubber.[120] The use to which this was put is unfortunately not mentioned, but the statement as it stands indicates a possible aboriginal practice.

The Otomí are the principal people of the semi-desert plateau for whom the existence of the ball game can be established, but there are indications that other tribes adjacent to the higher culture centers of central Mexico may also have received it. Thus, Vivó, following Kirchhoff, states that the Guachichil, northern neighbors of the Otomí, possessed such Meso-American traits as the *teponaztli*, *pulque*, and the ball game.[121] If the latter be equated with the rubber-ball game, the Guachichil might equally have received it from the tribes of the east coast and the Sierra Madre Oriental, from the Otomí, or from the Tarascans to the south. Until further information is at hand, the present data must be regarded as insufficient for proof of the presence of the rubber-ball game in the central portion of the North Mexican Interior Plateau.

Data for the east coast are likewise scanty, although sporadic indications point to the probable existence of the game there. For the Huastec, Meade states that the native word for ball, *mule*, suggests that the rubber ball was known, together with the associated sport.[122] In addition, he indicates on the basis of surface appearances that archeological courts may be present in the Huasteca, although none has yet

y Molina, cited as a source by Blom, gives the following pertinent words: Bola: *Na núnni* (p. 26); Juego: *Nahéy, théy*, (p. 57); and Jugar: *Héy* (p. 58). He does not list an equivalent for ball or ball game, though Yepes (p. 208) lists: Pelota: *Núnni gudu...* (orthography simplified here).

[119] Noguera, 1946, p. 344 (translation mine). Lámina 72 shows views of the two courts at Toluquilla. In the first court, a man standing on the bench gives an approximate height for the rear wall of ca. 8–10 feet. The wall appears to be in batter.

[120] Altamirano, 1906, p. 1100.

[121] Vivó, 1946, p. 326.

[122] Meade, 1942, p. 141.

been excavated. To the north, Tamaulipas yields only a passing reference to a game called *pelota*.[123]

North of Tamaulipas, the Gulf littoral gives no evidence of the rubber-ball game, and it is probable that neither the game nor a trade in rubber ever extended into the southeastern United States. The Natchez on the lower Mississippi did, however, have a hand-ball game, played at the harvest festival; and Beals has pointed out similarities it bears to the Mexican rubber-ball game.[124] It is undeniable that parallels do exist: the ball must not touch the ground, the surface of a cabin forms a goal for each side, and a prize is awarded to the victors. It is possible that fundamental resemblances are masked by the differences in play arising from the non-resilience of the stuffed ball employed. While not minimizing the force of such arguments, I prefer at present to follow Swanton in considering the hand-ball game of the Southeast as a variant of lacrosse,[125] the relationship of which to the rubber-ball game will be discussed in the final section.

For the west coast, on the other hand, detailed ethnographic and archeological materials are available. There the game has survived into the present. Clavigero, writing in the latter part of the 18th century, stated that, while it was no longer played in the Mexican empire, the ball game persisted among the Nayarit, Opata, Tarahumare, and other nations of the north.[126] It may be added that it seems to have had a continous distribution in this area. For Jalisco, in the region inhabited in historic times by Aztecoid (Cazcan ?) peoples, there is a brief reference which indicates its presence there.[127] We have a recent, comprehensive report from Nayarit, to be cited below, which describes the game and indicates its survival in adjacent areas, together with a brief, recent note from Mocorito, Sinaloa. Finally, there are early accounts of its occurrence among the Cáhita of Sinaloa and Durango.

Notably lacking, however, is any evidence supporting Clavigero's statement that the game was known to the Opata and Tarahumare. A probable explanation lies in the remark by an acquaintance, countryman, and fellow-priest, Father Gilij, who indicates that the information in question was based in part on hearsay.[128] Moreover, each is known to

[123] Beals (1932, table 74, p. 188) citing Alejandro Prieto, *Historia y Estadística del Estado de Tamaulipas* (Mexico, 1873). Prieto (p. 124) mentions the games of *pelota* and *la carrera*; the latter, Beals identifies as the kick race.

[124] Beals, 1932, Table 74, p. 188.

[125] Swanton, 1946, pp. 680 — 1.

[126] Clavigero, 1917, vol. 2, p. 215.

[127] Beals (1932, table 74, p. 188) citing *Noticias varias de Nueva Galicia* (Guadalajara, 1878, p. 357). In the Tegualtiche-Cazcan region, one of the vices is a game called *pelota de ule* or *juego de nalgas*.

[128] Gilij, 1781, vol. 2, bk. 4, ch. 16, p. 272.

possess the kick race, in which a ball is also employed; and hearsay might easily confuse it with the game which Clavigero reported.[129]

It must be acknowledged that the discrepancy between Clavigero's statement and the testimony of other observers *might* arise from a dynamic circumstance, in which the kick race moved in to replace the rubber-ball game in the favor of Tarahumare and Opata. A number of reasons have, nonetheless, led me to reject this alternative.

Detailed accounts are thus available only for Nayarit, Cáhita, and Acaxee, although an additional note is at hand for the town of Mocorito and further research will doubtless bring to light many other occurrences. In the following description, the four examples now available will be treated together for purposes of comparison. Throughout, it must be borne in mind that the Cáhita, Nayarit, and Mocorito loci lie in the lowlands, though the latter partakes somewhat of the piedmont, while the Acaxee occupied the highlands. Moreover, three hundred years separate the Nayarit and Mocorito accounts from those bearing on the other two peoples, during which time both European and central Mexican influences must have exerted strong pressure for change.[130]

Game: The recent occurrence of the ball game has been limited to the

---

[129] Bancroft, it is true, describes (1882, vol. 1, pp. 586–7) the rubber-ball game for the Opata, and, as is his wont, lists references *en bloc* for a whole page of text. His first reference is Ribas, p. 15, and his entire description, with minor exceptions, agrees with the account given there, so that it is difficult not to see in Ribas the original of his passage. Ribas, however, is talking not about the Opata, but about the Cáhita of Sinaloa. Although I have not yet checked all the other sources listed by Bancroft, I feel justified in denying to the Opata the pleasures of this sport. I might add that Beals (1932, table 76) allows them only the kick race.

[130] Sauer, 1934, *passim*. The Cáhita appear to have retained the game up to relatively recent times, judging from the statement of Lloyd (1911, p. 5) that W. H. Stayton, a captain in the U. S. Navy, on duty in the Gulf of California observed Yaqui Indians playing a game with a ball twice the diameter of a baseball, which they threw from hip to hip.

Nayarit: Kelly, 1943, pp. 163–171.

Cáhita (and adjacent tribes ?): Ribas, 1645, bk. 1, ch. 4, p. 15; for vocabulary, Buelna, *passim*. These data are well summarized by Beals (1943, pp. 34–73), who adds additional details.

Acaxee: Santarén, quoted in Alegre (vol. 1, bk. 4, pp. 405–7) and paraphrased in abridged form by Ribas (bk. 8, ch. 3, pp. 475–6). The latter adds information not found in Alegre: Ribas, bk. 8, ch. 7, p. 486. All of this material may be found in Beals, 1943, pp. 11–13.

What may possibly be an additional source for the Acaxee is given by Gumilla in the course of his discussion of the Otomac game, in a citation of P. (for Padre ?) Rojas, *Historia Cinaloa*, lib. 8, cap. 3, fol. 475. This work appears to be unknown today and I have been unable to locate it. It must be pointed out, however, that book, chapter, and pagination are identical for Ribas' passage on the same subject, raising the suspicion that Gumilla himself is in error.

Mocorito Village: Judd, 1940, p. 432.

Acoponeta valley of Nayarit; in Sinaloa, to the Mazatlan district in the south, to the Mocorito River, and on the Rio Sinaloa in the north; while reports already cited place it inland in Jalisco, in the vicinity of Teocaltiche. Chavero, in annotating Camargo, remarks that it then (1892) formed one of the most popular sports in Sinaloa and Sonora.[131]

In Nayarit, the name, *hulama*, is applied to the game itself (cf. Nahuatl *ulamaliztli*) and Chavero asserts that in his boyhood the same term was applied to the Sinaloa ball court.[132]

Ball: The Nayarit call it *hule*, the Cáhita, *ulin*. For them, and for the Acaxee as well, the resin of which it is made (Cáhita, *ulle*) comes from a tree. Kelly adds for the Nayarit certain details of manufacture: the gum comes from trees growing in the coastal country, is coagulated with certain herbs, and amassed in small increments until a ball has been formed. Like the Cáhita and Acaxee product, the Nayarit and Mocorito ball is solid. Size and weight vary: a Nayarit example has an average diameter of about seven inches and weighs about eight pounds, the Mocorito ball is three inches in cross-section, while the Acaxee ball is described as combining the size of a man's head with a weight of from two to three pounds. The Cáhita example was large and dense enough to be lethal on occasion.

When not in use, the Nayarit ball is suspended in a bag and is turned frequently to preserve its shape. The Mocorito villagers place their ball in a two-piece wooden mold between games.

Court: For both Nayarit and Cáhita, i.e. the inhabitants of the tierra caliente, the court is only a special plaza. The Nayarit *taste* (cf. Nahuatl *tlachtli*) is a rectangle 2.3 to 2.8 m. in width and approximately 11.3 to 14.0 m. long, delimited by four markers, of stone or brick, or by wooden pegs set flush with the ground, one at each corner. Two additional markers, similar to the others, are placed in the center of each of the two longer sides. Between the corner markers the rectangular plan of the court is then traced in the dirt, using the foot, and a similar, center line, *analco* ("on the other side of the river") is drawn between the two median markers. The zones behind the end lines are known as *chiche*.

The Cáhita court, which is only described as a flat, clean-swept plaza, was called *batei*, a name which, as we have seen (fn. 2, chapter III), was carried from the Antilles into Mexico by the Spaniards. The same term *(vatey)* seems to have been applied to the Acaxee court. Since a cognate appears in Cáhita with an associated meaning,[133] it appears that the term reflects native usage. It may, accordingly, be pertinent that the

[131] Muñoz Camargo, 1892, p. 136, note 2.

[132] *Ibid*, p. 136, note 3.

[133] Beals, 1945, p. 44: "The sticks used in the stick race are called *kuta bateyimteyeunaki*. The word *batéy* apparently refers to the older ball-game court."

two tribes in question speak a language far more removed from Nahuatl than that spoken in Nayarit.[134]

The impromptu game witnessed at Mocorito was played on "a long, narrow field... marked off in the plaza."

The Acaxee court, so Father Santarén tells us, was the first thing built in a town; a statement which is suggestive of a central location. It consisted of a small plaza, very flat, and with walls at the sides a *vara* (about a yard) in height, in the manner of a bench.[135] It does not seem likely that the feature alluded to as a "bench" in connection with the central Mexican courts is here described. Information is lacking as to terminal lines or other features of the court. The unexpected visit of a missionary while a game was in progress revealed an image in the form of a man placed on one side of the court and a peyote root on the other. This practice strongly recalls the setting of the images of two deities upon the walls of the central Mexican court.

Players: Only men are spoken of as taking part in the games of Cáhita and Acaxee, and this is true today for Nayarit and doubtless for Mocorito as well. The Acaxee selected their best players to represent them in inter-community games. In Nayarit, a man might organize a team, feed it, and supervise its practice even to the point of whipping an inattentive player.

Protective equipment seems to have been lacking for the Cáhita players, judging by the statement that he struck the ball with the "bare

[134] See Mason and Johnson, which I have followed throughout. For this region, Sauer is basic.

[135] ". una plazuela muy llana y con unas paredes á los lados de una vara en alto á modo do poyo.." (p. 405). The description of Ribas which appears to be an abridgement of Santarén, speaks of the plaza as being "muy bien dispuesta, limpia, y cercada con sus ballados, a modo de tapias" (p. 475). Such a description could, of course, be applied to the Southwest courts, and it would surely be significant were the Acaxee court of this type. That it was not, and that we must prefer the statement of Santarén is indicated, not only by the facts already stated, but by archeological finds made in regions adjacent to that inhabited by the Acaxee.

Thus Mason found at Sotolitos and at Los Fresnos, sites located in Durango within the territory of the neighboring and related Xixime, structures which he thus describes: "These consist of an open depressed oblong court or plaza bounded on each side by a long mound of stones. The ends of the court are open and the level depressed area extends as an apron beyond the flanking stone mounds. The resemblance to a primitive type of Mexican ball-court is obvious" (Mason, 1937, p. 142 and fig. 4, c).

In the vicinity of Copala, within the sierras and lying southwest of the structures found by Mason, Sauer and Brand report finding a rectangular plaza, about 75 by 100 feet in measurement, with two stone walls, still breast high, bounding it. It is mentioned here, not necessarily as a true court, but to indicate the native conception thereof: its local name is "the ball court of the ancients" (Sauer and Brand, p. 26).

muscle" of the hip; and the same may have been true for the Acaxee for whom definite information is not available. The modern Nayarit, however, wear the counterpart of the Aztec girdle. This is a belt *(chimal)*, 10 to 15 cm. in breadth, made of the root fiber of a fig tree or of bark. Inside the belt is a leather pad. The whole device is laced in front with leather thongs, which are drawn together until the player feels "light". Aside from the belt, the player wears only a breech clout. His feet are bare; and gloves are not reported. At Mocorito the player protects his upper arm, with which he usually strikes the ball, with a bandana wrapping.

Pre-game conditioning: Prior to a game both Acaxee and Nayarit players were subjected to certain disciplinary measures. Thus, when the former were about to engage in an inter-village match, they selected players to represent the community and prepared them for the game. Beals infers that preparation took the form of special practice or of religious ceremonials.[136] As we shall see, the participation of the players in the last night of the pre-game ceremony, when they must dance through the night, can best be explained in terms of ritual purification and spiritual fortification.

Nayarit conditioning takes the form of dietary injunction. On the day of the game, or the first day, if it runs for several, only liquids, particularly milk, may be taken. In addition, players must remain at home, must observe continence, and directly after the game they must bathe.

We lack information about the Cáhita, save that, since they sweated vigorously in the course of play, all participants refreshed themselves by bathing in the river when the game was over. Here, as with the people of Nayarit, the practice is in part referable to the humid climate of the tierra caliente.

Teams and play: For all four peoples, equal sides are the rule. Teams numbered four, six, or eight among the Cáhita, five or more for the Acaxee; while in Nayarit five, and in Mocorito four, comprise the usual team. Among the Acaxee an exception to the general rule of equality arose when one village challenged several: the defending team of six or seven chosen players might have to meet the combined champions of all the villages that picked up the gage.

The Nayarit team places one player by the center line, another *(golpeador)* on the back line, and the three other players cover the court between them. An umpire *(juez)*, there may sometimes be two, rolls the ball into the court. A player recovers it with his hand and throws it into the opposing court. It may be returned direct or upon the first bounce. In any case, it must be struck only with hip or thigh to within four fingers of the knee. Players hurl themselves down to retrieve a low ball,

---

[136] Beals, 1933, p. 12.

leap for a high ball. If the center player returns the ball on the serve, without touching the center line, his side may invade the rival court; the purpose which this serves is obscure.

The Cáhita observed somewhat similar rules of play. The ball must not be touched with the hand, but only with shoulder and bare hip. Struck in this manner, it might fly thirty or forty paces. When it landed, the player closest to it was supposed to return it. I ow shots seem to have been taken with the hip, leaving us to infer that the shoulder might be preferred for high drives. Players often died from receiving the ball in the stomach.

Our authorities tell us little about the actual manner of play followed by the Acaxee, save that only the right shoulder and the hips might be employed in striking the ball. Here, too, enthusiasm sent players aloft after high shots or sprawling after ground grazers.

In the Mocorito game, the ball "was struck sometimes by the hip but usually by the bandanna-bound upper arm. Hit in this latter manner, the ball frequently was propelled forty or fifty yards."

Scoring: The modern Nayarit adhere to a somewhat complicated form of scoring that, in its intricacy, appears to have borrowed from some European cognate of tennis. This is not true of the manner in which scores are gained, which accords with information for other versions of the game. A point is counted when an opponent commits a body fault, touching the ball with other than the prescribed part of hip or thigh; when the ball goes dead in the rival court; or when, bouncing therein, it goes over the back line. A ball that passes over the back line without first bounding in the opponents' court is dead and must be replayed. To some degree, the back line would appear to serve as a goal, though this function is not entirely clear.

Two methods of service are employed. The *golpeador* of the side that has scored calls the number of points his team has won and puts the ball into play. If the number is 1, 4, or 5, he bounces the ball, touches it to hip, and throws it overhand *(arriba)* into the rival court. If the score is 2, 3, 6, or 7, he rolls it *(male)* to the opposing side.

It is in the complex system of scoring that extraneous elements seem to crop up. Scoring is double: the team that scores adds a point, while its opponent drops one. Certain minor exceptions to this general rule occur. Thus a team with three points, on losing two consecutively, drops the third as well; and similarly a team with seven, losing four in a row, loses all. The winning total seems normally to be eight points, although there is evidence that another figure might be agreed upon beforehand. There is no single play whereby the whole game can be won.

In comparison with the foregoing, the few rules that have come down to us from the Cáhita appear simple indeed, though this is no doubt illusory, resulting as it does from an incomplete account of the game.

We know only that the body fault existed, since a point was lost if the ball was touched with the hand. In addition, the major objective of play was to send the ball across the end line defended by the opponents. Although we are told that such a play won the wager, it is more probable that a point system was involved, the total being chosen before the game, since otherwise points won from body faults would be meaningless.

For the Acaxee, even less is known. The body foul (touching the ball with an invalid part of the body) was in force, but just what the offending player lost, whether a point or the game, is not stated. Information as to goals or methods of scoring are lacking.

Wagers: Heavy betting (Cáhita – *hatte*, to bet on games) was an invariable accompaniment of the ball game. Among the Acaxee, it became more intense during intercommunity games. Primarily, only individual property, in the form of clothing, ornaments, weapons, and the like, were wagered among the Acaxee, regardless of the importance of the game. When the Indians began working in the mines, village stakes rose as high as five hundred pesos.

Intervillage games were initiated when one Acaxee community, having selected its players, amassed its stake, in later days amounting to more than five hundred pesos, and sent it, on the backs of messengers, to three or four pueblos, challenging them and naming the day of the game. A pueblo to whom the dare had been given had to accept and put up its own stake. All the articles wagered were brought back by the messengers to their village. We have no data as to the method of dividing a stake that had been won, and no doubt it was a complicated affair. An additional touch was added by what seems to have functioned as a consolation prize. This was a feast prepared the day before the game by the women of the receiving pueblo, upon which, if the home team won, all dined. In the case of a defeat, the host community consoled themselves by refusing a mouthful to their victors.

Nayarit women might take part in the betting itself; and this may have been generally true for the Acaxee and Cáhita as well.

Religio-ceremonial associations: A predilection on the part of the people of Nayarit to hold games on feast days may reflect some religious association; but it is as readily explicable on other grounds. For the Cáhita, information is lacking. On the other hand, Santarén gives us an excellent description of the pre-game ceremony of the Acaxee which I translate literally. It takes place upon the return of the messengers with the stakes:

> Then the people of the challenging village clean the *vatey*, so that not a pebble remains: this done, three days before the contest, all the men and women of the village dance in the *vatey*. In this manner, on the first night, two Indians prepared and accoutered for war, go out upon the walls of the

vatey, whence they give several cries, and then the old men and youths emerge from concealment in an arbor and proceed in complete silence up to the center of the *vatey,* where they begin to sing loudly. When the women hear this they come forth in the same way, and when they are all together, they dance for three hours, singing of all the merits and reasons they have to rejoice. The next night they do the same thing, and the words they sing are in praise of their players, applauding them and extolling their spirit and nimbleness, and thus they pass another three hours of the day..... The last night, the eve of the appointed day, they go out to dance as in the two pre-ceding days, and those who are to play next day are obliged to be there from nightfall till dawn without stopping singing or dancing. This night they sing of the strength of the enemy, of their cunning and grace in play, inspiring their own players and urging them on for the struggle.

When the day has come, if the padre is in the village, they observe respect by waiting until the mass is over before making their entrance. Otherwise, they begin in the morning, and their entrance is in this fashion. The two soldiers go forth as on the preceding nights, stripped for war and fully armed with lance and shield, and when they have taken their place upon the walls, the men enter as before to dance, and then the women. When they are all together, there enter through one side of the plaza the challenged villages, readied as for war, and begin to shoot blunt arrows at the two men on the walls, throwing balls of nettles, thistles, and thorns at them, from which they must try to protect themselves, since they are naked. They would suffer from it, did they not shield themselves so well; but since their foes are many, they abandon the plaza. When they have gone, together with those who have been dancing, the plaza falls to the enemy; but they enter it once more in favor of those who are withdrawing. Those who are in the village, in order to play, make their entrance with great din and uproar and push the foe back out of the plaza. When the latter have left, there enter those who have been picked to play for them, who, on entering, throw the ball into the plaza. Each one takes his place without making up for the advantage in number of individuals, since the six or seven from the village are obliged to play against all those who come forth for the other side, although they may be three and four, or double the number.[137]

Surely, nothing could more explicitly delineate the pattern of hostility thus transferred to the sphere of the game!

Additional religious practices of the Acaxee are suggested by an incident related by Ribas: a priest, unexpectedly entering a village in which a game was in progress, found an image in human form and a peyote root atop the walls of the court. Such images, important in the religion of the Acaxee, often formed the personal fetishes of individuals.[138] Ribas says of peyote: "although it is a medicinal, yet in its use there are many superstitions, which the Holy Tribune of the Inquisition had at times to punish."[139] In this instance, the father launched forth into a sermon which so moved his listeners that they destroyed the idol, "the demon within it," as well as the court itself.

[137] Alegre, 1841, pp. 405–6.
[138] *Vide* Beals, 1933, pp. 22–6.
[139] Ribas, 1645, p. 486.

Brief mention may be made here of a game played by the present-day Cáhita and described by Beals:

> Not mentioned by ancient sources, yet because of its non-European flavor meriting description here, is a game now called pelota, but very different from other games to which that generic name is applied. It is played with a rubber ball, slightly smaller than that used for *ule* or the surviving type of Mexican ball game, which is generally known south to Jalisco. A guard is worn on the right forearm, and it is a foul if the ball touches any other part of the body. The playing field is marked out by two lines about six feet apart. A center line divides the two parts but there are no back lines to the 'courts.' The ball must be returned within the court boundaries but may touch the ground. It is usually caught on the fly and bounced on the ground to return it. From one to four men play on a side, taking positions one behind the other if there is more than one player, or adopting a 'staggered' formation... Each side has a judge or *veedor* (Sp.), who keeps score either by scratching on the ground with a stick or writing on a piece of paper. The game is won when either side gets twenty-one points but if the score is tied at three points or any mutiple thereof, such as six or nine, all the scores are wiped out and the game starts over again. Consequently it is customary for games to start at dawn and not to end until evening, if then. What seems of special significance is that games are played between villages and heavy bets are placed on the outcome. The game is played from a little above Guasave on the Sinaloa to Culiácan and it is commonest around Guasave, Nio, Bamoa, Mocorito, and Tamazula... [it is] played mostly by Mexicans [but they were] Indians a few generations ago. I only observed practice games; there may be more formalization in the serious intervillage contests.[140]

It is quite likely that this game is another form of the one also described by Judd for Mocorito, though the brevity of his note makes it difficult to reach a conclusion. In the use of forearm for striking the ball there is a suggestion of European influence, just as in the Judd account a growing preference for the upper-arm (formerly shoulder?) as against the hip may be visible. As Sauer points out, Spanish forces early disrupted native culture in much of Sinaloa.[141] Material already cited in the course of the present paper indicates that European ball games were introduced shortly after the Conquest, and undoubtedly they borrowed such features as the rubber ball from native games.

In the present instance, not only the method of striking the ball with the forearm, but also some of the basic methods of play and the form of scoring suggest European modifications, although all of them may not have been introduced at the same time. The prestige of things European in the process of I adinization, together with the fundamental resemblance between the two types of game may well have been operative in their incorporation. Heavy betting and the presence of scorekeepers are common to both; intervillage games and day-long play are specifically indigenous.

Discussion: Comparison between the three chief northern Mexican versions of the aboriginal ball game reveal closer relationship between

[140] Beals, 1943, pp. 36–7; see also fig. 7.   [141] Sauer, 1932, pp. 1–2.

Cáhita and Acaxee than between either and Nayarit. To some extent this may reflect temporal differences: the processes of culture change seem to have brought to the Nayarit game a breakdown of community participation, together with a certain standardization and a more complicated method of scoring. On the other hand, it is precisely this area which through the years has retained the protective belt and has specialized in striking only with hip and thigh, the fashionable manner of central Mexico. To the north, both shoulder and hip are used and protective equipment is lacking. Professional players, specifically absent among the Acaxee, and probably so for the Cáhita, are prominent in Nayarit.

The indicated absence of the structural court in the lowlands cannot be attributed merely to the absence of an architectural tradition, for stone houses were known among both the Yaqui and the Tepic, as well as the Acaxee.[142] Again the apparent lack of ceremonialism in the early Cáhita game is perhaps attributable to the brevity of the description, and there seems little doubt that whatever religious association the Nayarit game may once have possessed has now vanished. As against Acaxee and Nayarit, Cáhita seems to have laid little stress upon intervillage competition. In the kicking race, the latter tribe, we are told, might muster two hundred players,[143] and a whole town might be split into two competing teams.[144] Such a moiety arrangement does not of necessity preclude intercommunity games as well; but it provides an alternative competitive duality that may diminish emphasis upon such contests. Incidentally, Ribas states of the kicking race that it served to exercise the tribes for war.

Taken together, the northern Mexican versions of the game reveal positive differences from their central Mexican counterpart. The court, where it exists, is less complex, lacking such features as bench, end walls, and rings. Among the Cáhita the function of the latter as goals may have been transferred to the terminal line. Equipment does not include gloves, save in the modern, putatively altered, Cáhita game. While the average size of the team may be comparable, the minimum number of players on a side is less for the Valley of Mexico. Wagers, perhaps reflecting the lesser concentration of political power in the north, as well as demographic factors and economic concepts, are less thoroughgoing in nature.

When the rules of play in the Nayarit, Acaxee, and early games are compared, it is at once evident that there are basic and far-reaching resemblances with the areas to the south. The body fault appears in all three, scoring by sending the ball over the opponent's back line in

---

[142] Beals, 1932, pp. 107–110, and pertinent maps and tables.

[143] Ribas, 1645, p. 15.

[144] Cf. the Opata, who also chose teams along moiety lines (Bandelier, Part I, p. 240).

Nayarit and Cáhita, and scoring on a ball that has died in the rival court in Nayarit. Fuller information for the other two would doubtless corroborate the Nayarit data. Variants of these rules appear again in central and southern Mexico, and some form of the dead ball in the Maya area. These methods of scoring appear to form a pattern that antedates the development of a center marker into the paired rings of the classic central Mexican game. Once this is realized, similarities between the entire Mexican (Mexico-Maya) sphere and those of Central and South America at once take on a more intimate character.

Further comment will be deferred until the concluding section.

The Southwestern United States

The most northerly extension of the rubber-ball game thus far recorded lies within the state of Arizona, where the archeological culture known as the Hohokam exhibits both a ball court and the rubber ball.[145] The Hohokam sites are centered in the drainage of the Gila and Salt Rivers, in the southern part of the state, but extend into adjacent portions of Sonora as well, where Ekholm found a court at Santa Cruz. To the north of the nuclear region, Hohokam influences carried the court into the Verde Valley and into the Flagstaff area in the northeastern corner of Arizona.

Two types of court exist in the Hohokam. The earlier, "Snaketown" type is oriented east-west, and has a modified double – "T" plan with rounded ends. It makes its appearance in the Colonial and early Sedentary Periods at Snaketown, at an estimated time of 600–900 A. D.[146] In the Sedentary Period (ca. 1000 A. D.) it is replaced at that site by the second class of court, termed "Casa Grande." This is oriented North-South, lacks end zones, and is approximately a quarter as long as the "Snaketown" court.[147] To date it has been by far and away the more

---

[145] The present discussion relies heavily upon basic reports by Haury (1937a) and McGregor, and upon the able summary of Chard. In a recent paper, published since the above was written, Schroeder adds to the number of reported courts and offers an appraisal of the significance which these structures hold for Southwestern prehistory, a view which stresses the organizational qualities their construction implies and the probability of religio-ceremonial associations.

Of the two rubber balls thus far recovered from the Southwest, only one now survives (Lloyd), to be the subject of reports by Amsden and by Haury (1937), the latter including the findings of chemical analysis.

[146] These dates derive support from cross-finds of pottery from the Anasazi area at Snaketown, and are thus not subject to the same measure of criticism as has been directed at Gladwin's dating for the earlier phases.

[147] Average dimension (Gladwin et al, vol. 1, p. 45):

	Overall Length	Interior Length	Interior Breadth
Casa Grande	25–30 meters	22 meters	10 meters
Snaketown	120 meters	56 meters	19 meters

common type of court in Arizona. Both courts are surrounded by adobe walls the inner face of which slopes steeply to the ground. No bench is present, nor is there any indication of the existence of rings. To be sure, Hewett does relate to the ball game certain stone rings found by him in the Casas Grande region of Chihuahua and in the cliff-dwellings of the Pajarito Plateau,[148] but it is doubtful that they had any connection with the game. Nor need rings be postulated, in view of their general absence in northern Mexico.

Perhaps the most striking feature of both forms of court is the presence of alley markers, sometimes one, but more frequently three, ranging down the center axis of the court. Present knowledge of the distribution of alley markers places them principally in the Maya and southern Mexican regions, and the example, previously referred to, in the Codex Nuttall might bring it somewhat further north. There remains however a vast gap in central and northern Mexico to be accounted for. It is quite possible that in those areas the markers may have been subfloor deposits, like many of those in the Southwest, and so have been overlooked by early writers. To some extent, too, they may have been replaced in those areas by the lines traced in perishable materials on the floor of the court. Whatever the answer may be, the findings in Arizona clearly indicate the antiquity of alley markers within the sphere of Middle American developments.

Two rubber balls have thus far been discovered in the Hohokam area, neither in association with a court. One of them was subjected to chemical analysis, the results of which revealed the desert shrub, *guayule*, as the probable source of the rubber. It was solid and, now distorted in shape, it has a maximum diameter of 86 mm. (3.4 in.). The finding of these balls greatly strengthens the identification of the ball courts as such. Chard entertains reservations as to the type of game played in the courts, and it is of course possible that the game may have undergone a "sea-change" in its new environment. Moreover, his caution is justified, in view of the distance of the areas he is comparing: Maya and Southwest. In the light of the evidence now at hand, it appears valid to contend that a game of the general northern Mexican type was introduced into Arizona by the colonial Hohokam.

Between the southernmost of the southwestern courts and the most northerly of the Mexican examples (the Acaxee court) there lies a provocative gap of some four hundred miles. In the coastal lowlands, to be sure, the Cáhita are somewhat closer to the Hohokam; but as Kelly points out "prepared" (i. e. walled) courts have not been reported along the coast from the Colima-Michoacan border to northern Sonora.[149] Such courts, on the other hand, do appear in the adjacent highlands, which

[148] Hewett, 1943, p. 159.   [149] Kelly, 1943, p. 173.

furthermore present additional features in common with Hohokam. That archeological reconnaissance and excavation will bring to light additional highland courts to fill the gap is to be anticipated. On the other hand, the highlands may have been occupied too late to form the bridge along which Mexican traits passed to the Southwest.[150]

Discussion: The significance for the larger picture implicit in the southwestern courts and associated findings is three-fold: 1) historically, it serves to validate hypotheses of Mexican influence in the Southwest; 2) from the ecological viewpoint it provides an instructive example of the adaptation of a tropical-forest development to a desert environment; and 3) in the early dates assigned to what is geographically a peripheral manifestation, it underscores the probability of the antiquity of the rubber-ball game in the Americas.

[150] *Ibid*, p. 174: Cf. discussion by Haury, 1945.

CHAPTER FIVE

CONCLUSIONS

The Game and its Distribution

It is generally the hope of the scientist that when he has brought together enough materials he may put them together into a factual structure which, added to the edifices of other workers, will permit him to view the land which lies about him in better perspective. He is duty-bound however to test his materials for soundness before he incorporates them into the unit, lest it deposit him or his colleagues rather too suddenly upon the ground. In all frankness, the trustworthiness of the present structure is somewhat impaired by certain inherent defects. Chief among them is the unevenness of the various accounts in respect to fullness of reporting, which restricts their adequacy for comparative purposes. Coupled to this is the weakness inherent in negative information, well exemplified in the case of the Witoto: for whom Whiffen, despite a residence among them, makes no reference to the ball game, leaving its initial description to Farabee a few years later. It is, therefore, unwise to regard the present distribution as final. Additional facts will undoubtedly be supplied for the tribes already discussed, and other tribes may be added to the list. It is likewise quite possible that some instances already available may have eluded me. Finally, the occurrences here set forth are far from being simultaneous, for they range from the Maya of the Initial Series Period, one and a half millenia ago, to the modern Nambikuára, apparently just now taking over the game from their Paressí neighbors.

The fundamental fact of the relationship of rubber-ball games in North and South America, as already pointed out, has been accepted since the early years of the Conquest. Analysis, however, shows that there are really two fundamental types of rubber-ball game which in the form of the ball and in the method of its manufacture, indicate some sort of linkage, genetic or otherwise, but which do not form sociological equivalents, appearing at times in complementary roles within the same social pattern.

The simpler form embodies play only for the self and may actually contain no competitive principle: as a correlary, it flourishes principally as a domestic sport and is frequently played by women as well as by men. In it, players arrange themselves in a circle (it is, therefore, here called circle game) and strike the ball aloft with hand or foot, seeking to prevent it from touching the ground.

In the second type of game, which forms the major subject of this paper, the emphasis is upon aggressiveness and the game is truly competitive. Players as a rule are able-bodied men, although in rare instances and under special rules of play, women may participate.[1] Contests between two teams, often representing different communities, are characteristically accompanied by heavy wagers and, when the ball is solid, by possible danger to life. The game takes place in the central plaza or within a specially prepared court, of which each team defends one half. Only prescribed portions of the body may be used in striking the ball, as, head, shoulder, hip, knee; and ordinarily the use of the hands is specifically enjoined.[2] Points are normally scored upon a body fault, a shot that passes the rear boundary, or one that dies in the rival court. The winning number of points is agreed upon beforehand, although in a few cases the scoring of a special goal wins the game outright. Tension may be overtly manifested in taunts and jeers; while officials often serve to diminish friction over disputed plays or scoring.

If the manner of play, which is inherent in the use of a resilient ball, is ignored, fruitful comparisons can be made between the two types of game and other games in North and South America. Typologically, the circle game must be considered an aspect of games similarly played, which occur widely throughout the Tropical Forest and Eastern Marginal areas of South America in the guise of the maize-leaf-ball game, appearing again among the Botocudo and Fuegians in a variant played with a skin- or bladder-covered ball.[3] The rubber ball of the circle game is reported specifically from the Mojos-Chiquitos culture area, where it appears side by side with the competitive type of rubber-ball game; and it is likewise present within the Guianas, the adjacent Northwestern Marginal area, in the Montaña,[4] and among the Ge-speaking marginals of eastern Brazil.[5]

[1] In the only stated instances, the Otomac and Taino, it is known of the former at least that the women accompanied their menfolk into battle.

[2] In three instances, namely, a tribe of the Uapés-Caquetá region, the Colorado, and the Cavina, games of catch are described. In each instance there is strong reason for suspecting alien influences in the game which lead to their exclusion from the discussion of the aboriginal forms that follows. Since, however, we possess only a passing mention for the latter two occurrences, it would be premature to set them permanently apart.

[3] Maize-leaf-ball games: Nordenskiöld, 1919, p. 160, map 29; Botocudo: Wied-Neuwied, 1820–1, vol. 2, p. 42; Fuegians (Yahgan): Cooper, 1946 a, p. 100.

[4] See Steward, (1948 c) for the classification of culture areas within the Tropical Forest.

[5] It is possible that the team game of the Apinayé may be historically unrelated to the competitive game of the western Tropical Forest, from which it is at present isolated. The use of battle dores and the conversion of one ball into a shuttlecock, the latter feature found again among the related Sherente, are elements suggestive of the simpler circle game. While other divergencies from

Outside South America, similar games are rarely mentioned. However, dictionaries of Middle American languages frequently contain terms referring to ball games, otherwise undescribed, in which the ball is struck with the hand or knee. On lexical grounds, they are distinguishable from the competitive rubber-ball game, the name for which frequently contains the morpheme for rubber. The use of hand or knee in striking the ball forms by itself far too feeble a basis to support an identification of the Middle American games with the South American circle games.[6] The Landívar account shows how forms can arise which are apparently intermediate. In North America, noncompetitive ball games of any sort have a limited, sporadic distribution.[7]

To the major rubber-ball game, embodying team play, North America provides numerous parallels, for competitive ball games are almost universal there; and lacrosse, shinny, and the kicking race present a continuous distribution which, in the case of the latter at least, overlaps the northern limits of the rubber-ball game in Mexico and the Southwest. At its southern extremity, on the other hand, hockey appears in the Gran Chaco contiguous to it and indeed presents close similarities, while log-racing (Ge) and *pillma* (Araucanian and, subsequently, Patagonian) show less obvious resemblances. It seems arguable that the striking correspondences evinced by shinny, lacrosse, and hockey, arise from an historical relationship: that they represent diversified, widespread descendants of a ball-and-stick game that was ancestral as well to the competitive rubber-ball game.[8]

---

the competitive pattern might, indeed, be ascribed to the ceremonial milieu in which the Apinayé game occurs, it is not likely that they reflect basic differences: that here the example of team rivalry in log racing along moiety lines may have transformed the circle game into a form superficially resembling the more complex team game.

[6] In at least one instance (Tzeldal) the game of hand ball is described as a European introduction, very probably one of the trio, *paume, pallone,* and *pelota.* How far this may also hold for the cognate games reported by other dictionaries is uncertain.

[7] Culin, 1907, pp. 561 f.

[8] North America: Culin (1907); Korn (n. d.); Swanton, 1929, 1946; Beals, 1932, table 76. In lacrosse, competing teams, comprising players equipped with one or two racquets, strive to carry or throw the ball to a goal at the opposing end of the field. In a variant form in the Southeast, the ball is struck with the palm instead of a racquet (Swanton, 1946, pp. 680–1). Usually the contest is between communities, moieties, or tribes. At times the winning number of points is agreed upon beforehand. Referees are present and betting is heavy.

Shinny differs from lacrosse chiefly in that the ball is struck along the ground with a bat. It usually shows less complex societal associations.

The kicking race is played by teams which race, usually over a prepared course, each team kicking a ball or billet as it goes. Betting is prominent and intercommunity matches frequent.

Forms of hockey resembling shinny are described for central Mexico (Beals

Within the compass of its occurrence, the latter ranges from the southwest of the United States, through the Mexican culture area (north, central, and southern Mexico and the Maya region), in the circum-Caribbean (both on the mainland and in the Antilles), within the Tropical Forests of South America east of the Andes (chiefly in those areas denoted Northwestern Amazon, Montaña, Western Marginal, Mojos-Chiquitos, and the southern section of the Madeira-Tapajóz region) as well as among the adjacent southern Amazon Marginal peoples and the Guaraní of southeastern Brazil.

The most prominent feature of this incidence lies in the concentration of the game within the Tropical Forest, in which it appears almost exclusively about the headwaters of the Amazonian tributaries. Yet it may be questioned whether this distribution represents the entire picture. For example, the apparent absence of any form of circle game (maize-leaf ball or otherwise) and of team game (rubber ball) in reports from the Tupian areas of the lower Amazon basin and the Brazilian littoral may well reflect the early cultural disintegration of the coastal Tupi and the hostility and consequent inaccessibility of their Amazonian congeners.

Nevertheless, the striking distribution of the team game within the Tropical Forest region, based on present knowledge, cannot be dismissed on what are merely presumptive grounds. Its absence throughout much of central and eastern Brazil in particular invites further inquiry. From a purely historical point of view, it may be argued that the game must have passed by riverine routes to its present position. If one considers that the total drainage of the Amazon was involved, the absence of the game in the middle and lower reaches may bespeak considerable antiquity for the survivals on the peripheries formed by the upper Amazon-

and Carrasco) and may be depicted at Teotihuacan (Acosta and Moedano Koer).

Chaco: Métraux, 1937, p. 398f. Hockey, as already mentioned, corresponds roughly to shinny in manner of play. A full account is to be found in the article cited, a summary by the same author (1946, p. 334). Intercommunity play is frequent, referees are present, and the winning score is agreed upon prior to the game.

Ge: Nimuendajú (1946, pp. 136–145 and Map 3) has described at length the log racing which forms the national sport of the Ge. It comprises relay races by teams, often drawn from competing moieties, each of which bears a log over a prepared course.

Patagonia: D'Orbigny (1835–47, v. 2, p. 85f.) describes in detail the Araucanian game of *pillma*, as it had been taken over by the Patagonians; and he even likens it to the rubber-ball game which he had previously described for the Chiquito. In *pillma*, which seems in reality to resemble the weapon duels of the southern Patagonians, two teams face each other within a circle traced on the ground. Paired players, one from each side, take turns in duelling with a pair of balls, each striving to throw it from beneath his left leg in such a manner as to strike his opponent and bounce out of the ring.

ian tributaries. An alternative suggestion on the same plane would bring the game along some such route as that pointed out by Palmatary, involving the Orinoco, the Casiquiara Canal, and the Rio Negro,[9] thus by-passing the lower Amazon completely as route of diffusion[10] and rendering less tenable arguments for age based upon geographical location.

Relations to Ecology and Culture

That the occurrence of th ecompetitive rubber-ball game is a direct function of ecological features is true at least in part, insofar as it occurs chiefly where sources of rubber are native. In the Chaco, it is found only on the northern margins (where the balls seem to have been imported); by and large, it is absent from the Andean Highlands; and in northern Mexico and the southwestern United States only the presence of a rubber-bearing desert shrub relieves the game from direct dependence upon the tropical rain forest. Yet within the rubber-producing areas, it was far from attaining its maximum potential extent: in the Guianas and eastern Brazil the rubber ball is indeed used, but only in the domestic circle game.[11]

The suggestion has, indeed, been made that the relative abundance of vegetal cover may have acted as a deterrent upon the expansion of the competitive variant, through the effort required to clear the space in which to play. Comparison with the general vegetation zones of South America[12] and with accounts by ethnographers of the physical environment of peoples known to possess the team game fails to indicate a direct correlation with relatively open country. Thus, only versions of the circle game employ the rubber ball in the gallery forests of Highland Brazil and in savanna and gallery forest areas of the Guianas. Within the lower course of the Amazon seasonal floods might be expected to discourage games requiring large cleared areas, but it is at least questionable that they would be prohibitive. The case for ecological determinants within the regions of native rubber is far from being conclusive; and accordingly it would be well to turn to an examination of the cultural factors that may have been operative.

It is evident, for one thing, that the competitive rubber-ball game is confined to peoples who for the most part are dependent upon agriculture for subsistence, although, to be sure, fishing and to a lesser extent

---

[9] Palmatary, 1939, p. 56.

[10] Steward (1947, p. 101) has recently commented upon these waterways in their relation to the transmission of circum-Caribbean culture elements within the South American Tropical Forest area.

[11] The game of the Apinayé, of eastern Brazil, has been discussed in fn. 5 above.

[12] Denis, 1927, Pt. 1, map: Formations végétales.

hunting may play an important supplementary role. Clearly, this must reflect demographic as well as economic determinants: relative permanency and size of settlement, together with a division of labor and a means of storing surplus foods to permit men the leisure to play together, must h ive predisposed a people toward maintainance of the game. In compai itively permanent villages, moreover, the area immediately adjacent o the houses is usually cleared, forming a plaza that can, on occasion, serve as a ball court.

With social institutions that might reflect the composition of the group that furnishes the ball team no correlation is yet evident: no regular linkage appears between the game and such structures as the patrilocal unit or the sib or moiety.[13] No more does it coincide, by and large, with the elaboration of class systems. There are, however, certain features in the societal environment which appear to favor the adoption of the game, and the game itself suggests what they should be. It is predictable that the sense of unity fostered by play against another group, as well as the cooperative patterns engendered in team activity, should have a fairly constant correspondence with an evolved political organization. This is actually the case, if the chieftainship be taken as an index of political development; but it is likewise true that the tribes that have the game exhibit a wide range in the degree of complexity to which this institution is brought.

Several associations are suggested, although the fragmentary nature of the information available may prevent them from becoming explicit. No correlation, either positive or negative, is yet manifest relative to boys' puberty rites, although the demands upon the manly skill and endurance of the participant suggest that the game may sometimes have functioned as an ordeal or demonstration of manhood. Systematic, aggressive warfare is practiced by only a few of the peoples that have the game, although war itself is known to all. It is no accident that strong parallels exist between warfare patterns and those of the competitive ball game (Map 6). Within the team, interpersonal relations are cooperative, but directed toward a highly competitive goal. Yet the individual has the opportunity to gain high prestige by his prowess. The pitting of teams from two communities against each other in a game in which hard-driving, dexterous action wins high stakes, frequently though not everywhere, at the risk of injury or death, all lead to the occasional substitution of the game for overt warfare. Undoubtedly, some of the translation of values arises from the recognition of the basic similarities cited on the part of the players, who are, at the same time, the warriors of the community.

[13] Games between moieties are specifically mentioned for the Kepikiriwat and Apinayé, and is suggested for the Chiquito by D'Orbigny's statement that teams were drawn from two halves of the village.

Interestingly enough, lacrosse in North, and hockey in South America appear occasionally to be considered in like manner as substitutes for war.[14] The compelling analogy presented by these similarities intimates that such competitive team games may often assume a sociological role of this character, secondary only to that of sportive diversion. Not only may games of this type be consciously employed on occasion to secure ends usually attained by fighting, but it may also function as a safety valve to relieve suppressed intercommunity conflicts, thus operating to sublimate belligerent tendencies and directing them into harmless action.

Yet another linkage has sometimes been proposed, namely with certain religious beliefs clustering about concepts of fertility.[15] That such associations may occur cannot be denied, but they are not as constant or widespread as was once believed. The appearance of the ball game in the course of ceremonials may actually be a function of the gathering together of large groups, sometimes from different communities, in festive mood, with leisure to participate and to watch. The Aztec game provides an instance in point, for there are indications that only with the growth of ceremonialism was the game drawn into its orbit. Whatever the individual history of each association of this nature, it is clear that there is no overall homogeneity in religio-ceremonial content that would permit the postulation of a powerful cult as the vector for the ball game in its spread.

The competitive game thus exhibits considerable stability in form over nearly fifty degrees of latitude (see maps), yet it can be said to be congruent with only a few societal features: namely, with agricultural communities possessing at least a moderate degree of political integration, in which it serves as a sport, as well as a vehicle whereby youths may demonstrate their prowess and warriors maintain bellicose values even in time of peace. These are the general features that must have had weight in the adoption or rejection of the game. In addition, other local circumstances, such as tribal prestige and ceremonial linkage, may have been operative on occasion. At times, the acceptability of the ball game may have rested simply upon its diversional character. Finally, the picture at times must have been complicated by the rival attractions of other contestual games. Thus among the Ge-speaking marginals of eastern Brazil the log race is the chief competitive sport and there the rubber-ball game exists chiefly in the circle variant.

[14] Lacrosse (Creek): Swanton, 1928, p. 460. Hockey (Mataco): Métraux, 1937, p. 398f.; 1946, p. 334.

[15] See e.g. Spinden, 1933, p. 259f.

A Tentative History of the Rubber-Ball Game

The speculative digression of the past few pages will have justified itself if it has succeeded in clarifying some of the more important elements in the physical and social environment that have entered into the total distribution of the rubber-ball game. Reserved for final consideration is the temporal factor; and implicit in such an inquiry is a reconstruction of the past history of the game. A discussion ot this sort is by the very nature of the data bound to be highly conjectural, yet it may bring into focus aspects that at first glance do not appear to be associated.

Resemblances between games in North and South America have been remarked before:[16] and it seems reasonable to assume that the development cf the resilient ball merely led to a modification of preexisting patterns of play, to which it became assimilated. In one line of incorporation, the ball was drawn into the circle game, which on several counts can be considered ancient in South America; while along another route it took on the form of the competitive game. The two variants can only be said to have taken form after the rubber ball, with its special rules of play, had become integrated within the earlier framework. Their evolution consequently cannot be determined by reference to the antiquity of the prototypical games, which may have had a long history prior to assimilation of the new elements. No more can their age relative to each other be assessed, for they may have been largely independent in development.

Any attempt to deal with the dissemination of the competitive rubber-ball variant must inevitably attempt to delimit the locus of its origin. In theory, the game might have taken form anywhere within the area in which it is found today (it is improbable that any people dependent upon trade for rubber would have evolved it) and it is so thoroughly adapted to the tropical rain forest that it is probable that it originated there. Within this far-flung vegetation zone, there are two contenders for primacy, namely the combined Mexican (Mexico and Maya) and circum-Caribbean (Central and northwestern South America and the Antilles) areas, and the Tropical Forest area of South America. The point at stake is thus the direction in which the game diffused, with implied reference to the donor-receptor relationship in other shared traits.

Claims for the antiquity of the rubber-ball game in South America are supported by several characteristics of variable weight. The distribution of the competitive game has already been dealt with: claims for great age based upon a present distribution peripheral to the main drainage of the Amazon are set aside if an alternate route of travel from

[16] Cooper, 1942, p. 26; 1949.

the Orinoco and up the Rio Negro is postulated. Arguments which take their root in the greater variety of rubber-ball games in South America are subject to the objections offered in discussing the origin of the variant forms of game. There remain for examination, factors having to do with the elaboration of the rubber ball and of t'ie game itself.

The relatively high development in the technology of rubber within the Amazonas region of South America may be cited as offering a favorable environment for the development of the rubber ball, although the solid type which demands no such evolved processes, might easily have been created in any locality in which rubber was utilized. On the other hand, the relative distribution of the more complex hollow form (Map 2) suggests that, if the two types are directly comparable, it is a later and secondary invention, restricted to South America alone. Since, from the point of view of form and principle of manufacture, the hollow rubber ball seems to bear a close relationship with the rubber syringe bulb, it may actually have had a long existence apart from the ball game.[17] Nonetheless, as a specialized and integrated feature it has a certain measure of weight in favor of a South American origin.

Finally, in the combination of body parts with which the ball is struck, the Tropical Forest area shows a far greater heterogeneity than do the regions to the north (Map 3). When examined in detail, however, the several instances resolve themselves into groupings about what may be considered secondary centers of elaboration. These are two in number: namely, the Mojos-Chiquitos area, together with the surrounding regions, in which the use of the head is stressed, with lesser emphasis upon shoulders, legs, and elbows; and the Montaña-Northwest Amazon center, which formalized use of knees and feet.[18] In comparison with the homogeneous pattern of play to the north, in which the use of the hips is the rule, and shoulder and knee occupy a subordinate position, the variation within the Tropical Forest, even when it is reduced to two patterns, conveys a certain amount of persuasiveness in arguments for a South American development of the game. Yet such differences may rest in the degree of compulsion toward standardization on the part of the

[17] Nordenskiöld, 1917, p. 85; 1930, pp. 54, 62. Nordenskiöld has suggested (1930, p. 63) that the molding of the hollow rubber ball may have inspired the development of casting à cire perdue, which can be placed in the cultural sequences of the Highlands. Attempts to obtain a minimal dating for the game from the first appearance of this technique would come to grief on twin objections: that the direction of the postulated influence has not really been established, and that the ball may have had a history independent of the game.

[18] It has been suggested that a correlation may exist between the use of the head and the occurrence of the hollow ball. They are not unassociated, to be sure, but the correspondence is equivocal: an equal number of tribes using the head employ solid and hollow types of ball.

societies concerned: a factor which if established, would tend to vitiate the force of even that argument.

The case for a South American origin must accordingly be set aside as unproven, rather than as finally untenable. Yet even its chief proponents appear to have thought in terms of a development in the northern portion of the continent, for they speak of the Arawak migrations as having been responsible for carrying the ball game into the Antilles and Middle America, as well as south into the area of the Tropical Forest.[19] The validity of this view is somewhat impaired by the present evidence that Tupi-Guaraní tribes equal or perhaps surpass in number the Arawakan groups within the total that possess the game. In the upper reaches of the Amazon there is, indeed, some indication that Tupian peoples may have been the local vehicle of dispersion.

Yet the evidence that has been marshalled in proof of influences from the north, of which the ball game forms a prominent member, cannot be brushed aside. Deferring for a moment the identity of the vectors, let us consider the claims which the areas to the north can advance.

Arguments for the primacy of Middle America rest more upon the demonstrable antiquity of Maya courts and those in the Southwest than upon great variation in the form of the game. The proponents for South America may be hard put to furnish similar testimony from the Tropical Forest area, in view of the absence of structural courts there. The nature of the game, and of the court used, is such as to leave little that might serve to indicate the former presence of the game. Depiction of a game is almost the sole evidence that can be expected, barring accidental preservation of a ball. Under known circumstances, it is hazardous to argue that archeological silence in the Tropical Forest is tantamount to a denial of antiquity.

A discussion of the claims in favor of the circum-Caribbean is more fruitful. Since we possess descriptions for only two tribes from this area, the Taino and the Otomac, we are doubly fortunate in having several accounts for each. In a number of characteristics relating to the game they show special resemblances not shared by other peoples and these serve to emphasize their close cultural relationship. And yet, between them they possess, for example, the structural court, so highly elaborated within the Middle American zone, together with the use of the hip in striking the ball. The participation of large numbers of players and the stress, among the Otomac, upon employing the head, point toward the South American forms. The intermediate position of the circum-Caribbean tribes is still further indicated by the distribution of methods of scoring (Map 4) and the location and elaboration of ball courts (Map 5).

[19] Nordenskiöld, 1920, p. 108; Lothrop, 1937, p. 27; Schmidt, 1943, p. 19. See also Kidder, p. 446, for the view of a South American source.

The characteristics of the competitive rubber-ball game that have been passed under review suggest an original form involving a solid rubber ball, a generalized pattern of play, a form of scoring entailing the body fault and the ball dead in the opponents' field, a non-structural court, probably centrally located with reference to the community, together with basic aggressive values. These characteristics are best exemplified by the circum-Caribbean occurrences, although they are by no means impossible to distinguish elsewhere. The indications favoring a circum-Caribbean origin[20] have a fair degree of probability; but they are not decisive. In view of the long history behind the game and the great distance separating its extremes, the stability it evidences becomes all the more striking, and is explicable only in terms of a social environment that everywhere presented strong basic resemblances. This in itself is one of the weightiest arguments for a source within the Formative stages of the circum-Caribbean.

[20] See Steward, 1947, for a general statement on the relationship between Meso-American and other cultures. A fuller discussion by the same author will be found in Steward, 1948 d, pp. 1–15. Since this paper was completed, a major work has appeared on the subject in German by Dr. Walter Krickeberg (1948). Since both his paper and the present one cover much the same ground, although from different points of view, it is a matter of gratification to note that on many fundamental points they are in agreement. On other aspects, they dive, primarily in the assessment of the relative significance of the variables involved. As his title indicates, Krickeberg's central interest lies with the Mexican game, although he touches upon most of the other regions treated here. Since to incorporate or comment upon his views is impracticable at this time, it must suffice to call attention to the appearance of this paper.

BIBLIOGRAPHY

ACOSTA, JORGE R.
1940. "Exploraciones en Tula, Hgo.," *Rev. Mex. de Estud. Antrop.* IV : 3, pp. 172–194. Mexico.
1941. "Los últimos descubrimientos arqueologicos en Tula, Hgo. 1941," *Rev. Mex. de Estud. Antrop.*, V: 2–3. Mexico.

ACOSTA, JORGE R., and HUGO MOEDANO KOER
1946. "Los Juegos de Pelota," in *México Prehispanico* (Antologia de Esta Semana). Mexico. pp. 365–384.

ADAM, L., and V. HENRY
1880. *Arte y Vocabulario de la Lengua Chiquita.* Paris.

ALEGRE, F. J.
1841. *Historia de la Compania de Jesus en Nueva Espania.* 3 vols. Mexico.

ALTAMIRANO, F.
1906. "Datos para la historia y explotación del 'Guayule.'" *Boletin* de la Secretaria de Fomento (Segunda época), 5:10–I, pp. 1098–1123. Mexico.

AMSDEN, C. A.
1936. "A Prehistoric Rubber Ball," *Master key*, 10 : 1. pp. 7–8. Los Angeles.

APPUN, C. F.
1871. *Unter den Tropen.* Jena.

AUBIN TONALAMATL
see SELER, 1900.

BANCROFT, H. H.
1882. *The Native Races:* Vol. 1, Wild Tribes. San Francisco.
1886. *The Native Races:* Vol. 2, Civilized Nations. San Francisco.

BANDELIER, A. F.
1890–2. "Final Report of Investigations among the Indians of the Southwestern United States, carried on mainly in the years from 1880 to 1885," *Papers of the Archaeological Institute of America.* American Series III and IV. Cambridge.

BARKER, P. W.
1940. *Rubber: History, Production, and Manufacture,* Dept. Comm. Bur. For. & Dom. Comm., Trade Promotion Ser. 209. Washington.

BARRERE, P.
1743. *Nouvelle Relation de la France Equinoxiale.* Paris.

BASAURI, C.
1940. *La Población Indigena de México Etnografía.* Secretaría de Educación pública. 3 vols. Mexico.

BEALS, R. L.
1932. "The Comparative Ethnology of Northern Mexico before 1750," *UC-IA,* No. 2. Berkeley.
1933. "The Acaxee," *UC-IA,* No. 6. Berkeley.
1943. "The Aboriginal Culture of the Cáhita Indians," *UC-IA,* No. 19. Berkeley.
1945. "The Contemporary Culture of the Cáhita Indians," *BAE-Bull. 142.* Washington.

BEALS, R. L., and P. CARRASCO
 1944. "Games of the Mountain Tarascans," *AA*, n. s. 46:4, pp. 516–522.
  Menasha.
BELLO, W.
 1907. "Extracção de borracha," in *O Brasil, Suas riquezas naturaes, Suas*
  industrias. Rio de Janeiro. Vol. I, Primeira Parte: Industria extrac-
  tivareino vegetal, pp. 1–74.
BELTRAN, P.
 1859. *Arte del Idioma Maya*. Merida.
BLOM, F.
 1932. "The Maya Ball-game *Pok-ta-pok* (Called *Tlachtli* by the Aztec),"
  Middle Amer. Research Ser., Publ. 4. New Orleans.
BODLEIAN 2858
 See Kingsborough, E. K.
BOLLES, J. R.
 n. d. Unpublished notes on the Monjas court, Chichén Itzá.
BRASSEUR DE BOURBOURG, C. E.
 1851. *Popol Vuh*. Le livre sacré et les mythes de l'antiquité Americaine.
  London.
BUELNA, E.
 1890. *Arte de la Lengua Cahita*... Mexico.
BUENO, R.
 1933. *Apuntes sobre la Provincia misionera de, Orinoco e Indígenas de su*
  Territorio. Caracas.
CARBAJAL, A. L.
 1906. "Proyecto sobre la comunicacion de Chiquitos con el Paraguay
  (1788)," in Ballivian, M. V., *Documentos para la Hist. Geog. de la Rep.*
  de Bolivia, ser. 1, vol. 1, pp. 18–28. La Paz.
CARLI, G. R.
 1788. *Lettres américaines*. Boston.
CASO, A.
 1932. *La Tumba 7 de Monte Albán es Mixteca*. Mexico.
 1935. *Las Exploraciones en Monte Albán Temporada 1–34–1–35*. Instituto
  panamericano de Geog. e Hist., Publ. Num. 19. Mexico.
CERVANTES SALAZAR, F.
 1936. *Crónica de Nueva España*. Mexico.
CHANTRE y HERRERA, J.
 1901. *Historia de las Misiones de la Compañía de Jesús en el Marañon*
  español (1637–1767). Madrid. Quoted in Métraux, 1928.
CHARD, C. S.
 1940. "Distribution and Significance of Ball Courts in the Southwest,"
  Papers of the Excavators' Club, 1 : 2. Cambridge.
CHARLEVOIX, P. X. DE
 1733. *Histoire de l'Isle Espagnole ou de S. Domingue*. Amsterdam.
CHARNAY, D.
 1887. *The Ancient Cities of the New World*. New York.
CHAVERO, A.
 1887. *Historia Antigua y de la Conquista*, vol. 1 of México a Través de los
  Siglos (ed. V. Riva Palacio). Barcelona.
CHURCH, G. E.
 1912. *Aborigines of South America*. London.
CLARK, J. C.
 1938. *Codex Mendoza*. 3 vols. London.

CLAVIJERO, F. S.
    1917. *Historia antigua de Mexico.* Mexico.
CODEX BORBONICUS
    see Hamy, E. T., 1899.
CODEX BORGIA
    see Seler, E., 1906.
CODEX COLOMBINO
    see Junta Colombina, 1892.
CODEX FEJÉRVÁRY-MAYER
    see Seler, E., 1901–2.
CODEX FLORENTINO
    see Sahagun, B. de, 1905.
CODEX MAGLIABECCHIANO, XIII, 3
    see Nuttall, Z., 1903.
CODEX MENDOZA
    see Clark, J. C., 1912.
CODEX NUTTALL
    see Nuttall, Z., 1902.
CODEX RAMIREZ
    see Radin, P., 1920.
CONANT, J. B.
    1936. *The Chemistry of Organic Compounds.* New York.
LA CONDAMINE, M. DE
    1778. *Relation abrégée d'un voyage fait dans l'interieur de l'Amerique meridionale.* Maestricht.
CONZEMIUS, L.
    1932. "Ethnographical Survey of the Miskito and Sumu Indians, etc., *BAE-Bull. 106.* Washington.
COOK, O. F.
    1944. "Natural Rubber," *SmI-AR for 1943.* Washington. Pp. 363–411.
COOPER, J. M.
    1942. "Areal and Temporal Aspects of Aboriginal South American Culture," *Primitive Man,* XV: 1–2, pp. 1–38.
    1946. "The Yahgan," in Steward, 1946, pp. 81–106.
    1946a. "The Culture of the Northeastern Indian Hunters: A Reconstructive Interpretation," in *Man in Northeastern North America* (ed. F. Johnson), pp. 272–305.
    1949. "Games and Gambling," in Steward, 1949, pp. 503–524.
CORBETT, J. M.
    n. d. *Ball Courts and Ball Game of the Ancient American Indians.* Master's Thesis, Univ. of Southern Cal., June, 1939.
CÓRDOVA, J. DE
    1942. *Vocabulario Castellano-Zapoteco.* Mexico.
COVARRUBIAS, OROZCO, S. DE
    1673. *Tesoro de la lengua castellana, o española* (Vol. 2 of Del Origen y Principio de la Lengua Castellana, by B. Aldrete.) Madrid.
CRAWLEY, A. E.
    1914. "Pallone, Pelota, and Paume," *The Field,* vol. 123, suppl.: p. xviii. London. April 25, 1914.
CRESSON, F. M., JR.
    1938. "Maya and Mexican Sweat Houses," *A. A.* n. s., 40: 1 pp. 88–104. Menasha.
CULIN, S.
    1907. "Games of the North American Indians," *BAE–24th AR.* Washington.

DENIS, P.
 1927. *Amérique du Sud* (Tome XV of *Geographie Universelle*, published under the direction of P. Vidal de la Blache and L. Gallois.) Paris.
DIVERTISSEMENTS INNOCENS
 1696. *Divertissemens innocens*. La Haye.
DURÁN, D.
 1867–80. *Historia de las Indias*, etc. 2 vols. Mexico.
EDER, F. X.
 1791. *Descriptio provinciae Moxitarum in regno Peruano*. Budae.
EKHOLM, G. F.
 1946. "The Probable Use of Mexican Stone Yokes," *A. A.*, n. s., 48: 4, pp. 593–606. Menasha.
 1949. "Palmate Stones and Thin Stone Heads: Suggestions on their Possible Use." *Amer. Antiq.*, 15 : 1, pp. 1-9. Menasha.
ENCYCLOPAEDIA BRITTANICA
 1937. "Lawn Tennis and Tennis," *Encyclopaedia Brittanica*, 14th edn. (Anonymous.)
ESPASA, J. (HIJOS DE)
 1914–35. "Pelota," in *Enciclopedia Universal Ilustrada*, vol. 43. Barcelona.
ESPINOSA, G. DE
 1864. "Relación hecha por Gaspar de Espinosa, etc.," in *Col. de Doc. inéd.*, ser. 1, vol. 2, pp. 467–522, (ed. J. F. Pacheco et al.) Madrid.
FARABEE, W. C.
 1922. "Indian Tribes of Eastern Peru," *Papers Peab. Mus. Am. Arch. and Ethnol.*, vol. 10. Cambridge.
FERNANDEZ, J. P.
 1726. *Relacion historial de las missiones de los Indios, que llaman Chiquitos*. Madrid.
FEWKES, J. W.
 1907. "The aborigines of Porto Rico and neighboring islands," *BAE-25th AR*. Washington.
GATTEL, C. M.
 1790. *Nouveau Dictionnaire Espagnol et François*. Lyon.
GILBERTI, M.
 1901. *Diccionario de la lengua tarasca ó de Michoacan*. (ed. A. Penafiel). Mexico. (Originally printed in 1559).
GILIJ, F. S.
 1781. *Saggio di Storia Americana*. Roma.
GLADWIN, H. S., E. W. HAURY, E. B. SAYLES, and N. GLADWIN
 1937–42. "Excavations at Snaketown: Material Culture," *Medallion Papers, Gila Pueblo*, No. 25. Globe.
GOLDMAN, I.
 n. d. "Tribes of the Uápes-Caquetá Region," in Steward, 1948, pp. 763–798.
GÓMARA, F. L. DE
 1826. *Historia de las Conquistas de Hernando Cortés*. (ed. C. M. de Busta-mente; from Chimalpain translation of original into Mexican). Mexico.
 1877. *Hispania Victrix*, in Biblioteca de Autores Españoles, vol. 22. Madrid.
 1940. *The Conquest of the West India (1578)*. New York.
GOODE, J. P.
 1946. *Goode's School Atlas*, 1946 edition. New York.
GUMILLA, J.
 1745. *El Orinoco Ilustrado*. Madrid.

GUZMAN, ALONSO DE
    (1620). *Vocabulario en Lengua Tzeldal*. Ms. in Brinton Col., Library, Mus.
        of Univ. of Penna.. Title page includes the statement, "traslado el
        vocabulario el sobredicho Pᵉ. el año de 1620 años en la provincia
        de los tzeldales enel pueblo de taquin vitz."
HABEL, S.
    1878. "The Sculptures of Santa Lucia Cosumalwhuapa in Guatemala,"
        Smithsonian Contrib. to Knowl., 269, vol. 22, no. 3 Washington.
HALL, H. M. and LONG, F. L.
    1921. *Rubber-Content of North American Plants*. Carnegie Inst. of Wash.
        Washington.
HARRINGTON, M. R.
    1921. "Cuba before Columbus," *MAI, HF-INM, Misc. 17*. New York.
HAMY, E. T.
    1899. *Codex Borbonicus*. Paris.
HATT, G.
    1924. "Archaeology of the Virgin Islands," *Proc. 21st Internat. Congr.
        Amer.* pp. 29–42. The Hague.
HAURY, E. W.
    1937. "A Pre-Spanish Rubber Ball from Arizona" *Am. Antiq.*, 2: 4,
        pp. 282–288. Menasha.
    1945. "The Problem of Contacts Between the Southwestern United States
        and Mexico," *SJA*. 1:1, pp. 55–74.
HEATHCOTE, J. M.
    1890. "Tennis," in *The Badminton Library of Sports and Pastimes*, vol. 25
        London.
HÉRNÁNDEZ, F.
    1946. *Antigüedades de la Nueva España* (tr. by J. Garcia Pimentel). Mexico.
HERRERA Y TORDESILLAS, A. DE
    1726–30. *Historia General de los Hechos de los Castellanos en las.Islas i
        Tierra-Firme del Mar Océano*. Madrid.
HEWETT, E. L.
    1943. *Ancient Life in Mexico and Central America*. New York.
HISTORIA DE LOS MEXICANOS POR SUS PINTURAS
        see Radin.
HISTORIA TOLTECA-CHICHIMECA
        see Preuss and Menghin.
HUMBOLDT, VON A. and A. BONPLAND
    1852–3. *Personal Narrative of Travels to the Equinoctial Regions of America,
        during the years 1799–1804*. (tr. and ed. by T. Ross). London.
IM THURN, E. F.
    1883. *Among the Indians of Guiana*. London.
IXTLILXOCHITL, F. DE ALVA
    1891–2. *Obras históricas de Don Fernando de Alva Ixtlilxochitl* (publ. and
        annotated by A. Chavero.) Mexico.
JENA, L. S.
    1944. *Popol Vuh. Das Heilige Buch der Quiché-Indianer von Guatemala*.
        Stuttgart. Ibero-Amerikanischen Institut, Berlin: II.
JOYCE, T. A.
    1933. "The Pottery Whistle-Figurines of Lubaantun," Pres. Address,
        JRAI, vol. 63, pp. xv–xxv.
JUDD, N. M.
    1940. "Progress in the Southwest," in *Essays in Historical Anthropology
        of North America*, Smithsonian Misc. Col., vol. 100, pp. 417–444.

JUMELLE, H.
  1915. *Les cultures coloniales. Plantes a latex et a résines.* Paris.
JUNTA COLOMBINA DE MEXICO
  1892. *Homenaje á Cristóbal Colón.* Mexico.
KARSTEN, R.
  1924. "The Colorado Indians of Western Ecuador," *Ymer,* vol. 44 : 2,
        pp. 137–152.
  1932. "Ceremonial Games of the South American Indians," *Commentatio-
        nes Humanarum Litterarum,* Tomus III : 2, pp. 1–38. Helingsfor.
KELLY, I.
  1943. "Notes on a West Coast Survival of the Ancient Mexican Ball Game,"
        Car. Inst. *Notes,* vol. 1, No. 26, pp. 163–175. Washington.
KIDDER, A. II
  1940. "South American Penetrations in Middle America," in *The Maya
        and Their Neighbors,* pp. 441–459. New York.
KINGSBOROUGH, E. K.
  1831–1848. *Antiquities of Mexico.* London. (Bodleian 2858 is vol. 1, no. 4
        therein.) 7 vols.
KIRCHHOFF, P.
  n. d. "The Otomac," in Steward, 1948 b, pp. 439–444.
KORN, L. J.
  n. d. *The Distribution and Analysis of "Lacrosse" in North America.*
        Master's Thesis, Univ. of Penna., 1934.
KRICKEBERG, W.
  1948. "Das mittelamerikanische Ballspiel und seine religiöse Symbolik,"
        Paideuma, Mitteilungen zur Kulturkunde, Vol. 3, nos. 3—5, pp.
        118—190. Frankfurt am Main.
KROEBER, A. L.
  1939. Cultural and Natural Areas of Native North America," *UC-PAAE,*
        vol. 38, pp. 1–242. Berkeley.
LANDA, DIEGO DE
        see Tozzer, 1941.
LANDÍVAR R.
  1948. "Rafael Landívar's *Rusticatio Mexicana* (Mexican Country Scenes)."
        Translated by Graydon W. Regonos. *Philological and Documentary
        Studies,* 1 : 5, Tulane Univ. New Orleans.
LAS CASAS, B. DE
  1877. *Historia de las Indias.* Biblioteca Mexicana (ed. J. M. Vigil). 2 vols.
        Mexico.
  1909. *Apologética Historia de las Indias,* in Nueva Biblioteca de Autores
        Españoles, vol. 14 Madrid.
LEHMANN, W.
  1905. "*Les Peintures Mixtéco-Zapotèques,* etc.," *Journ. de la Soc. des Amér.,*
        n.s., vol. 2, pp. 241–280. Paris.
LÉVI-STRAUSS, C.
  n. d. "Tribes of the Right Bank of the Guapore River," In Steward, 1948 a,
        pp. 371–379.
LITTERAE ANNUAE
        Litterae Annuae of 1605. Quoted in Nordenskiöld, 1920.
LLOYD, F. E.
  1911. *Guayule* (Parthenium argentatum Gray) *A Rubber-Plant of the
        Chihuahuan Desert.* Carnegie Inst. of Wash. Washington.
LOPEZ YEPES, J.
  1826. *Catecismo y Declaracion de la Doctrina, Cristiana en Lengua Otomí.*
        Megico *(sic).*

LOTHROP, S. K.
    1923. "Stone Yokes from Mexico and Central America," *Man*, vol. 23,
        no. 58, pp. 97–8. London.
    1927. "Pottery Types, and Their Sequence in El Salvador," *MAI, HF-
        INM*, 1:4, pp. 165–220. New York.
    1937. "Coclé. An Archaeological Study of Central Panama," Part I: *Mem.
        Peab. Mus. Arch. and Ethnol., Harvard Univ.* vol. 7. Cambridge.
LOVÉN, S.
    1935. *Origins of the Tainan Culture, West Indies*. Göteborg.
MARBAN, P.
    1701. *Arte de la Lengua Moxa....* Lima.
MARONI, P. (probable author)
    1889–92. "Noticias auténticas del famoso Rio Marañon y Mission apostó-
        lica de la Compañía de Jesús de la Provincia de Quito en los dila-
        tados bosques de dicho rio," (publ. M. J. de la Espada), *Boletin
        de la Soc. Geog. de Madrid*, nos. 26–30. Madrid.
MARQUINA, I.
    1928. *Estudio Arquitectónico Comparativo de los Monumentos Arqueologicos
        de México*. Secretaría de Educación Pública, Mexico.
MARTINEZ, HERNANDEZ, J. (ed.)
    1929. *Diccionario de Motul Maya Español atribuido a Fray Antonio de
        Ciudad Real y Arte de Lengua Maya por Fray Juan Coronel*. Mérida.
MARTIUS, C. F. PHIL. VON
    1867. *Beiträge zur Ethnographie und Sprachenkunde Amerikas' zumal Bra-
        siliens*. 2 vols. Leipzig.
MARTYR D'ANGHERA, P.
    1944. *Decadas del Nuevo Mundo*. Buenos Aires.
MASON, J. A.
    1937. "Late Archaeological Sites in Durango, Mexico," *Twenty-fifth Anni-
        versary Studies* (ed. D. S. Davidson), Publ. Phila. Anthrop. Soc.,
        vol. 1, pp. 127–146., Philadelphia.
    1941. "A Large Archaeological Site at Capá, Utuado, etc,." in *Scientific
        Survey of Porto Rico and the Virgin Islands*, vol. 18, pt. 2. N. Y. Acad.
        Sci., vol. 18, part 2. New York.
MASON, J. A. and JOHNSON, F.
    1940. "The Native Languages of Middle America," and "The Linguistic
        Map of Mexico and Central America," respectively; in *The Maya and
        Their Neighbors*, pp. 52–88. New York.
McGREGOR, J. C.
    1941. "Winona and Ridge Ruin," *MNA-Bull. 18* 2 vols. Flagstaff.
MEADE, J.
    1942. *La Huasteca, Epoca Antiqua*. Mexico.
MENDIETA, G. DE
    1870. *Historica eclesiástica indiana (XVI Century)*. Mexico.
MÉTRAUX, A.
    1928. *La Civilisation Matérielle des Tribus Tupi-Guarani*. Paris.
    1937. "Etudes d'Ethnographie Toba-Pilaga (Gran Chaco)," *Anthropos*,
        vol. 32, pp. 171–194, 378–401.
    1942. "The Native Tribes of Eastern Bolivia and Western Matto Grosso,"
        BAE-Bull. 134. Washington.
    1946. "Ethnography of the Chaco," in Steward, 1946, pp. 197–370.
    1948. "The Guaraní," in Steward, 1948a, pp. 69–94.
MOLINA, A. DE
    1880. *Vocabulario de la Lengua Mexicana*. Leipzig.

MONTOYA, A. R. DE
  1876. *Arte de la Lengua Guarani, ó mas bien Tupi.* Vienna.
MORLEY, S. G.
  1922. "The Foremost Intellectual Achievement of Ancient America," *Nat. Geog. Mag.*, vol. 41 : 2, pp. 109–130. Washington.
  1937–8. *The Inscriptions of Peten.* Carnegie Inst. Wash., Publ. No. 437. 5 vols., Washington.
  1946. *The Ancient Maya.* Palo Alto.
MOTOLINIA (TORIBIO DE BENAVENTE)
  1903. "Memoriales de Fray Toribio Motolinia," *Manuscrito de la Col. del Sr. D. J. G. Icazbalceta.* Mexico.
  1941. *Historia de los Indios de la Nueva España.* Mexico.
MUÑOZ CAMARGO, D.
  1892. *Historia de Tlaxcala.* Mexico.
NEVE Y MOLINA, L. DE
  1767. *Reglas de Orthographia, Diccionario, y Arte de Idioma Othomi....* Mexico.
NIMUENDAJÚ, C.
  1939. "The Apinayé," *Anthrop. Ser. Cathol. Univ. Amer.*, No. 8 (tr. by R. H. Lowie). Washington, D. C.
  1942. "The Šerente," *Publ. F. W. Hodge Ann. Publ. Fund* vol. 4. Southwest Mus. Los Angeles.
  1946. "The Eastern Timbira," (tr. and ed. by R. H. Lowie), UC-PAAE, vol. 41. Berkeley.
NOGUERA, E.
  1946. "Culturas del Norte de Mexico," in *Mexico Prehispanico (Antologia de Esta Semana)*, pp. 331–9. Mexico.
NORDENSKIÖLD, E.
  1917. "Om Indianernes Anvendelse af Gummi i Sydamerika," *Geografisk Tidskrift*, vol. 24, no. 3, pp. 80–86. Copenhagen.
  1919. "An ethno-geographical analysis of the material culture of two Indian tribes in the Gran Chaco," *Comparative Ethnographical Studies:* 1. Göteborg.
  1920. "The changes in the material culture of two Indian tribes under the influence of new surroundings," *Comparative Ethnographical Studies:* 2. Göteborg.
  1922. *Indianer und Weisse in Nordostbolivien.* Stuttgart.
  1930. "Modifications in Indian culture through inventions and loans," *Comparative Ethnographical Studies:* 8. Göteborg.
NOTICIAS
  1878. *Noticias varias de Nueva Galicia.* Guadalajara. Cited in Beals, R. L., 1932.
NUTTALL, Z.
  1902. *Codex Nuttall.* Peab. Mus. Am. Arch. Ethnol., Harvard Univ. Cambridge.
  1903. *The Book of the Life of the Ancient Mexicans.* Berkeley. (Cod. Magliabecchiano XIII, 3.)
D'ORBIGNY, A. D.
  1835–47. *Voyage dans l'Amérique Méridionale*, Vol. 2. Paris. (9 vols.)
  1845. *Fragment d'un Voyage au Centre de l'Amérique Méridionale.* Paris.
OVIEDO Y VALDÉS, G. F. DE
  1851–55. *Historia general y natural de las Indias.* Madrid. (4 vols.)
PALCIO, E. J.
  1937. *Arqueologia de México, culturas arcaica y tolteca.* Mexico.

PALMATARY, H. C.
 1939. "Tapajó Pottery," Gothenburg Ethnographical Museum, *Ethnological Series:* 8, pp. 1–136. Gothenburg.
PARSONS, E. C.
 1945. *Peguche: A Study of Andean Indians.* Chicago.
PERAMAS, J. E.
 1793. *De vita et moribus tredecim virorum paraguaycorum.* Faventiae. Quoted in Métraux, A., 1928.
PÉREZ BAZÁN, T., and A. MANTEROLA.
 1936. *Disposiciones y Reglamento para el juego de pelota a mano, conocido con el nombre de "Pelota Mixteca."* Departamento de Educacion fisica. Oaxaca de Juarez.
PIO PEREZ, J.
 1866–77. *Diccionario de la Lengua Maya.* Mérida.
PONS, F. R. J. DE
 1806. *A Voyage to the eastern part of Terra Firma or the Spanish Main, in South America....* New York.
POPENOE, D. H.
 1936. "The Ruins of Tenampua, Honduras," *Sm. Inst. – AR for 1–35.* Washington, D. C.
PREUSS, K. T.
 1921–23. *Religion und Mythologie der Uitoto.* 2 vols. Göttingen.
PREUSS, K. T., and E. MENGHIN
 1937. "Die Mexikanische Bilderhandschrift Historia Tolteca-Chichimeca," *Baessler Archiv,* Beiheft 9. Berlin.
PRIETO, A.
 1873. *Historia y Estadistica del Estado de Tamaulipas.* Mexico. Cited in Beals, R. L., 1932.
(PRUDHOMME, L.) "L M B" on title-page.
 n. d. *Voyage a la Guiane et a Cayenne, faite en 1789 et Annees suivantes.* Paris.
RADIN, P.
 1920. "The Sources and Authenticity of the History of the Ancient Mexicans," *UC-PAAE,* vol. 17, no. 1. Berkeley.
RAINEY, F. G.
 1940. "Puerto Rican Archaeology," in *Scientific Survey of Puerto Rico and the Virgin Islands,* vol. 18, part. 1. New York Acad. Sci.. New York.
RAYNAUD, G.
 1925. *Les dieux, les héros et les hommes de l'ancien Guatémala, d'apres le livre de conseil.* Paris.
REAL ACADEMIA ESPAÑOLA
 1803. *Diccionario de la lengua castellana.* Madrid.
REYNOSO, D. DE
 n. d. *Arte y vocabulario en Lengua Mame dirigido,* Paris. Published by Count H. de Charencey, it is a reprint of the edition of 1644.
RIBAS, A. PEREZ DE
 1645. *Historia de los Trivmphos de Nvestra Santa Fee...* Madrid.
RONDON, C. M. DA SILVA
 1922. *"Conferencias Realizadas em 1910 no Rio de Janeiro e em S. Paolo.* Commissão de Linhas Telegraphicas Estrategicas de Matto Grosso ao Amazonas, Publicação n. 68. Rio de Janeiro.
ROOSEVELT, T.
 1914. *Through the Brazilian Wilderness.* New York.

ROQUETTE-PINTO, E.
1938. "Rondonia," *Biblioteca pedagogica Brasileira*. Serie 5ª, Vol. 39. S. Paolo.
ROTH, W. E.
1924. "An Introductory Study of the Arts, Crafts, and Customs of the Guiana Indians," *BAE-38th AR (1916–17)*, pp. 25–745. Washington.
ROUSE, I.
1942. "Archeology of the Maniabón Hills, Cuba," *Yale Univ. Publ. Anthrop.*, no. 26. New Haven.
RUPPERT, K.
n. d. Unpublished data on Court 3E2, Chichén Itza.
SAHAGÚN, B. DE
1905. Codex Florentino, illustrations to *Historia general*, etc. (ed. F. del Paso y Troncoso), vol. 5. Madrid.
1938. *Historia general de las cosas de Nueva Espana*. 5 vols.. Mexico.
SATTERTHWAITE, L.
1943–4. *Piedras Negras Archaeology Architecture*. Part. I, No. 1, Introduction; Part IV, Ball Courts. University Museum, Philadelphia.
SAUER, C. O.
1934. "The Distribution of Aboriginal Tribes and Languages in Northwestern Mexico," *UC-IA*, no. 5. Berkeley.
SAUER, C. O., and D. BRAND.
1932. "*Aztatlán*," *UC-IA*, no. 1. Berkeley.
SCHMIDT, M.
1912. "Reisen in Matto Grosso im Jahre 1910," *Zeit. f. Ethnol.*, vol. 44, pp. 130–174. Berlin.
1914. "Die Paressi-Kabishi," *Baessler Archiv*, vol. 4, pp. 167–250. Berlin.
1943. "Los Paressis," *Revista de la Soc. Cient. del Paraguay*, vol. 6, no. 1, pp. 1–296. Asunción.
SCHOMBURGK, R.
1922. *Richard Schomburgk's Travels in British Guiana, 1840–1844*. (tr. and ed. by W. E. Roth.) Georgetown.
SCHROEDER, A. H.
1949. "Cultural Implications of Ball Courts in Arizona", SJA, 5 : 1, pp. 28–36.
SCHULLER, R.
1935. "Das Popol Vuh und das Ballspiel der Ki'če-Indianer von Guatemala, Mittelamerika, *Internat. Archiv für Ethnog.* vol. 33, pp. 105–116. Leiden.
SELER, E.
1900. *Das Tonalamatl der Aubin'schen Sammlung*. 2 vols. Berlin.
1901–2. *Codex Fejérváry-Mayer*. London.
1902. "Der Codex Borgia und die verwandten aztekischen Bilderschriften," in Seler, E., *Gesammelte Abhandlungen zur Amerikanischen Sprach- und Altertumskunde* (1902–1923, 5 vols.), vol. 1, section 2; 1, pp. 133–144. Berlin.
1904. "The Venus Period in the Borgian Codex Group," in *BAE-Bull. 28.* (Mexican Antiquities), pp. 353–392. Washington.
1906. *Codex Borgia*. 2 vols. Berlin.
1908. "Einiges über die natürlichen Grundlagen mexikanischer Mythen," in *Gesammelte Abhandlungen*, etc., vol. 3, section 2, pp. 305–351. Berlin.
1923. "Mythus und Religion der alten Mexikaner," in *Gesammelte Abhandlungen*, etc., vol. 4, pp. 1–167. Berlin.

SHELFORD, V. E.
    1926. *Naturalist's Guide to the Americas*. Baltimore.
SNETHLAGE, E. H.
    1931. "Unter nordostbrasilianischen Indianern," *Zeit. f. Ethnol.*, vol. 62,
        pp. 111–205.
    1937. *Atiko y: Meine Erlebnisse bei den Indianern des Guaporé*. Berlin.
SOLIS, A, DE
    1844. *Historia de la Conquista de Méjico*, etc. Paris.
SPENCE, L.
    1923. *The Gods of Mexico*. London.
SPINDEN, E. S.
    1933. "The Place of Tajin in Totonac Archaeology," *A. A.*, n. s., 35: 2,
        pp. 225–270. Menasha.
SQUIER, E. G.
    1858. *The States of Central America*. New York.
    1869. "Tongues from the Tombs," *Frank Leslie's Illustrated Newspaper*,
        June 26, 1869. (No. 5 of a series of same title: it was for Central
        America.)
STAHL, A.
    1889. *Los Indios Borinqueños*. Puerto Rico.
VON DEN STEINEN, K.
    1894. *Unter den Naturvölkern Zentral-Brasiliens*. Berlin.
STEWARD, J. H.
    1946. "Handbook of South American Indians: Marginal Tribes," *BAE-
        Bull. 143* (Editor). Washington.
    1947. "American Culture History in the Light of South America," *SJA*,
        3 : 2, pp. 85–107.
    1948a. "Handbook, etc.: Tropical Forest Tribes," *BAE-Bull. 143* (Editor).
        Washington.
    1948b. "Handbook, etc.: Circum-Caribbean Tribes," *BAE-Bull. 143*, vol. 4
        (Editor). Washington.
    1948c. "Culture Areas of the Tropical Forests," in Steward, 1948a,
        pp. 883–899.
    1948d "The Circum-Caribbean Tribes: An Introduction," in Steward,
        1948b, pp. 1–41.
    1949 "Handbook, etc.: Comparative Ethnology of South American
        Indians," *BAE-Bull. 143*, vol. 5 (Editor). Washington.
STREBEL, H.
    1901. "The Sculptures of Santa Lucia Cozumahualpa, Guatemala, in the
        Hamburg Ethnological, Museum," *Sm. Inst. – AR for 1899*, vol. 1,
        pp. 549–561. Washington.
STRONG, W. D., A. KIDDER and A. J. D. PAUL
    1938. "Preliminary Report on the Smithsonian Institution – Harvard Uni-
        versity Archaeological Expedition to Northwestern Honduras, 1936,"
        Sm. Misc. Coll., vol. 97., no. 1. Washington.
SWANTON, J. R.
    1928. "Social Organization and Social Usages of the Indians of the Creek
        Confederacy," *BAE–42nd AR (1924–25)*, pp. 23–472. Washington.
    1929. "A point of resemblance between the ball game of the Southeastern
        Indians and the ball games of Mexico and Central America," *Journ.
        Wash. Acad. Sci.*, vol. 19, no. 14, pp. 304–7.
    1946. "The Indians of the Southeastern United States," *BAE – Bull. 137*.
        Washington.

TAPIA ZENTENO, C. DE
  1767. *Noticia de la Lengua Huasteca,....* Mexico.
TESSMANN, G.
  1930. *Die Indianer Nordost-Perus.* Hamburg.
TEZOZOMOC, H. A.
  1878. *Cronica Mexicana,* in Biblioteca Mexicana. Mexico.
THOMPSON, J. E. S.
  1933. *Mexico Before Cortez.* New York.
  1941. "Yokes or Ball Game Belts ?" *Am. Antiq.,* 6: 4, pp. 320–6. Menasha.
  1943a. "A Figurine Whistle Representing a Ball-Game Player," *Notes on
    Mid. Am. Arch. and Ethnol.,* no. 25, Carn. Inst. of Wash., Div. of
    Hist. Research. Washington.
  1943b. "A Trial Survey of the Southern Maya Area," *Am. Antiq.,* 9: 1,
    pp. 106–134. Menasha.
  1945. "A Survey of the Northern Maya Area," *Am. Antiq.,* 11: 1, pp. 2–24.
    Menasha.
THOMPSON, J. E. S., H. E. D. POLLOCK and J. CHARLOT
  1932. *A Preliminary Study of the Ruins of Coba, Quintana Roo, Mexico.*
    Carnegie. Inst. of Wash., Washington.
TORQUEMADA, J. DE
  1723. *Los Veinte i un Libros Rituales i Monarchia Indiana.* 3 vols. Madrid.
TOSCANO, S.
  1945. "Informe sobre la existencia de jugadores de pelota mayas en la
    cerámica escultórica de Jaina," *Notes on Mid. Am. Arch. and Ethnol.,*
    no. 54. Carnegie. Inst. of Wash., Div. of Hist. Research. Washington.
TOZZER, A. M.
  1928. "Maya and Toltec Figures at Chichen Itza," *Proc. 23rd Internat.
    Congr. Amer.* 1928. New York.
  1941. "Landa's Relación de las Cosas de Yucatan," *Papers Peabody Mus.
    Am. Arch. Ethnol., Harvard Univ.,* vol. 18.
VAILLANT, G. C.
  1944. *Aztecs of Mexico,* Garden City.
VAYTIA, M.
  1944. *Historia antigua de Mexico.* 2 vols. Mexico.
VILLACORTA, C., J. A. and F. N. RODAS
  1927. *Manuscrito de Chichicastenango (Popol Buj).* Guatemala.
VIVÓ, J. A.
  1946. "Caracteres de las culturas del Norte de Mexico," *Mexico Pre-
    hispanico (Antologia de Esta Semana),* pp. 323–330. Mexico.
VOCABULARIO
  n. d. *Vocabulario de la lengua Zoque.* Año de 1733. "Copiado de un MS. en
    posesion del Licenciado Don José Mariano Rodriguez, Tuxtla, por
    C. Hermann Berendt, M. D. Tuxtla Gutierrez, 1870." In Univ. Mus.,
    Univ. of Penna.
WHITBECK, R. H.
  1936. *Economic Geography of South America.* 2d ed. New York.
WHITMAN, M. D.
  1932. *Tennis Origins and Mysteries.* New York.
WIED-NEUWIED, M.
  1820–1. *Reise nach Brasilien in den Jahren 1815 bis 1817.* Frankfort a M(ain).
    2 vols.
XIMINEZ, F.
  1857. *Popol Vuh.* Vienna.

YDE, J.
    1938. "An Archaeological Reconnaissance of Northwestern Honduras,"
    Acta Archaeologica, vol. 9. Copenhagen.
ZORITA, A. DE
    1909. "Historia de la Nueva España, etc.," in *Col. de Libros y Doc. refer.
    á la Hist. de Amer.*, vol. 1. Madrid.

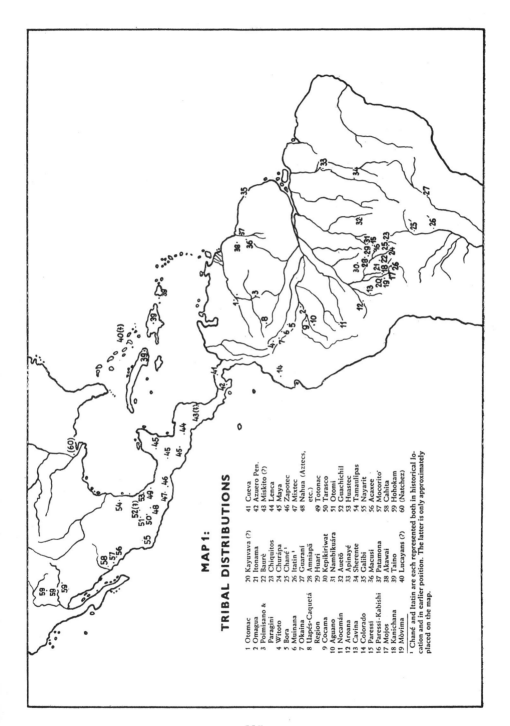

MAP 1:

TRIBAL DISTRIBUTIONS

1 Otomac	20 Kayuvava (?)	41 Cueva
2 Omagua	21 Itonama	42 Azuero Pen.
3 Poimisano &	22 Bauré	43 Miskito (?)
Paragini	23 Chiquitos	44 Lenca
4 Witoto	24 Churápa	45 Maya
5 Bora	25 Chané[1]	46 Zapotec
6 Muinana	26 Itatin[1]	47 Mixtec
7 Okaína	27 Guaraní	48 Nahua (Aztecs,
8 Uapés-Caquetá	28 Amniapä	etc.)
Region	29 Huari	49 Totonac
9 Cocama	30 Kepikiriwat	50 Tarasco
10 Aguano	31 Nambikuára	51 Otomi
11 Nocamán	32 Auetö	52 Guachichil
12 Aroana	33 Apinayé	53 Huastec
13 Cavina	34 Sherente	54 Tamaulipas
14 Colorado	35 Galibi	55 Nayarit
15 Paressi	36 Macusi	56 Acaxee
16 Paressi-Kabishi	37 Patamona	57 Mocorito'
17 Mojos	38 Akawai	58 Cahita
18 Kanichana	39 Taino	59 Hohokam
19 Móvima	40 Lucayans (?)	60 (Natchez)

[1] Chané and Itatin are each represented both in historical location and in earlier position. The latter is only approximately placed on the map.

115

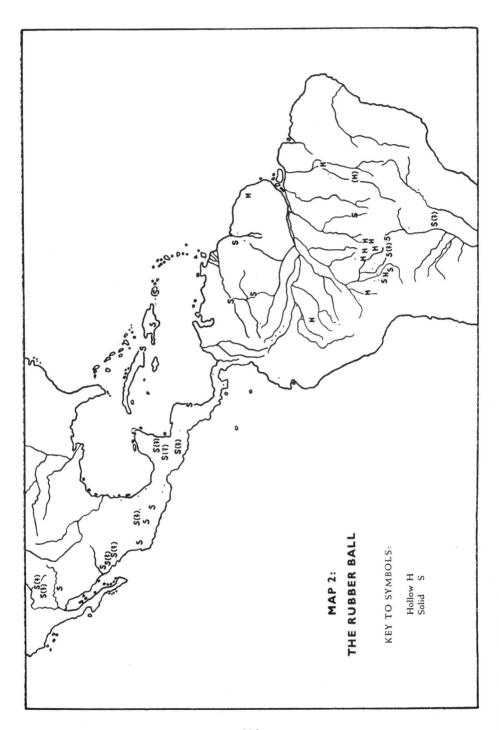

MAP 2:
THE RUBBER BALL

KEY TO SYMBOLS:

Hollow H
Solid S

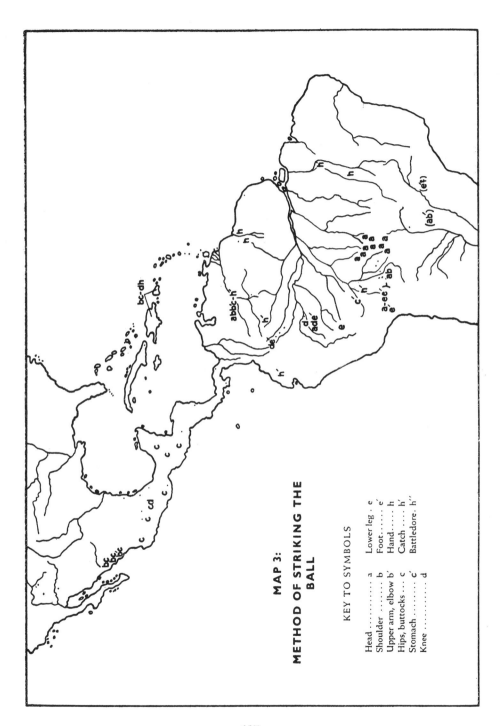

MAP 3:

METHOD OF STRIKING THE BALL

KEY TO SYMBOLS

Head . . . . a	Lower leg . . e		
Shoulder . . . . b	Foot. . . . . . e′		
Upper arm, elbow b′	Hand. . . . . . h		
Hips, buttocks c	Catch . . . . h′		
Stomach . . . . c′	Battledore. h′′		
Knee . . . . d			

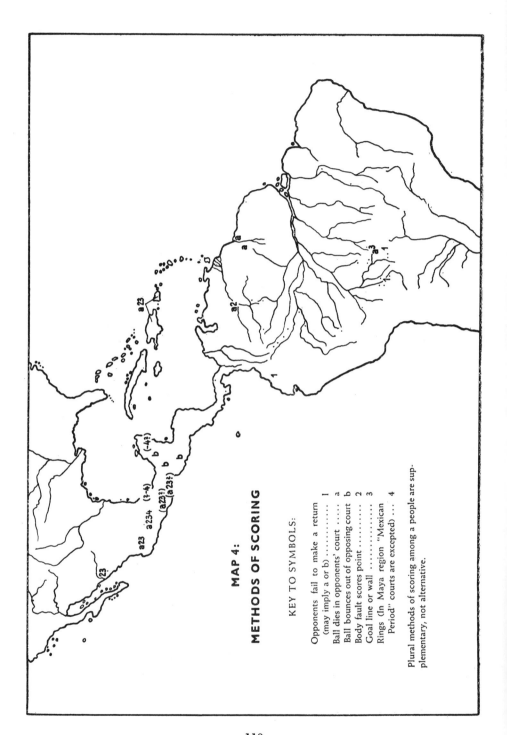

MAP 4:

METHODS OF SCORING

KEY TO SYMBOLS:

Opponents fail to make a return
(may imply a or b) 1
Ball dies in opponents' court ..... a
Ball bounces out of opposing court b
Body fault scores point 2
Goal line or wall 3
Rings (In Maya region "Mexican
Period" courts are excepted) ... 4

Plural methods of scoring among a people are supplementary, not alternative.

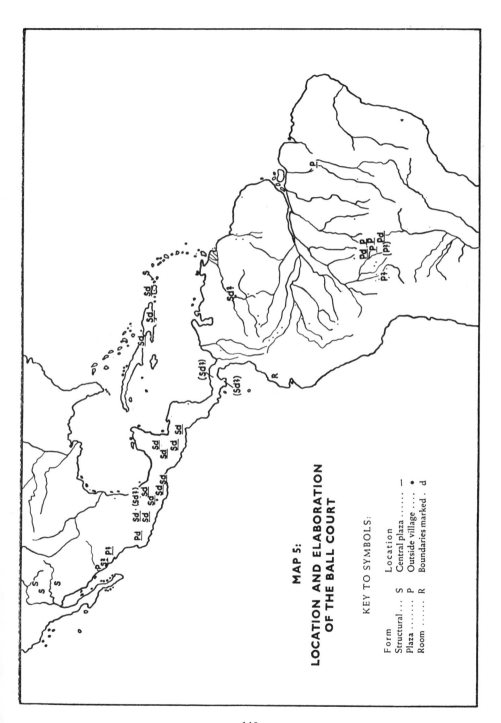

MAP 5:

LOCATION AND ELABORATION OF THE BALL COURT

KEY TO SYMBOLS:

Form		Location	
Structural	S	Central plaza	—
Plaza	P	Outside village	•
Room	R	Boundaries marked	d

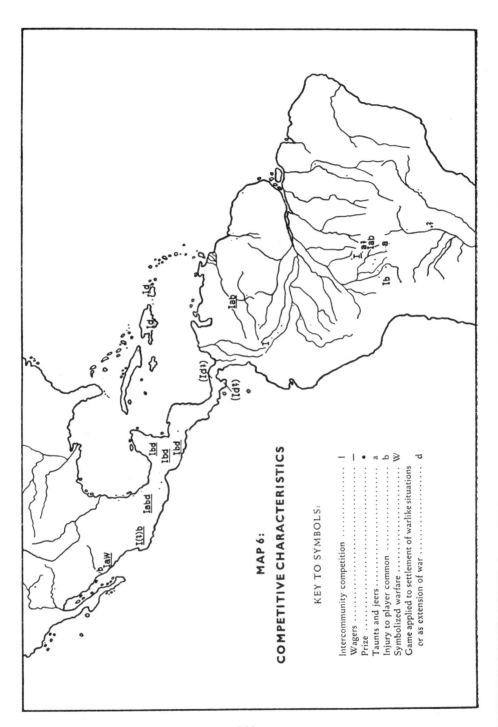

MAP 6:
COMPETITIVE CHARACTERISTICS

KEY TO SYMBOLS:

Intercommunity competition I

Wagers .... |

Prize .... •

Taunts and jeers .... a

Injury to player common .... b

Symbolized warfare .... W

Game applied to settlement of warlike situations
  or as extension of war .... d

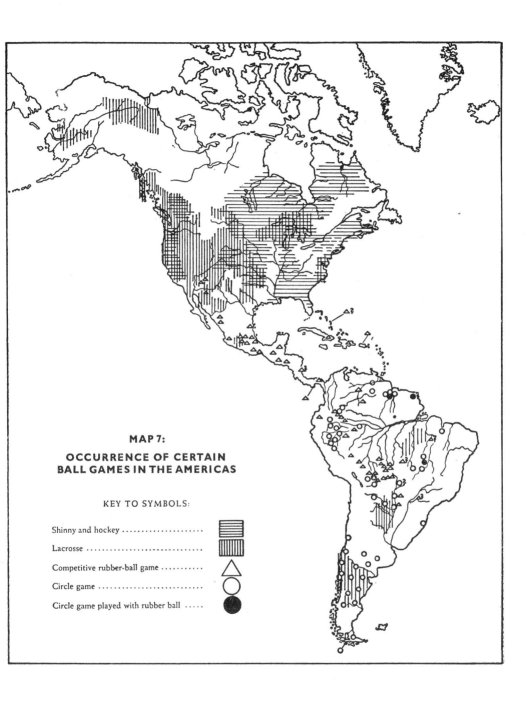

MAP 7:

**OCCURRENCE OF CERTAIN
BALL GAMES IN THE AMERICAS**

KEY TO SYMBOLS:

Shinny and hockey ....
Lacrosse ....
Competitive rubber-ball game ....
Circle game ....
Circle game played with rubber ball .....